Student Diversity

Classroom strategies to meet the learning needs of all students

FAYE BROWNLIE

CATHERINE FENIAK

LEYTON SCHNELLERT

2nd edition

Pembroke Publishers Limited

Dedicated to Gaby, Ben, and Cam,
whose learning regularly reminds us
to notice their individual pathways to success.
Each lesson they teach us makes us better teachers.

© **2006 Pembroke Publishers**
538 Hood Road
Markham, Ontario, Canada L3R 3K9
www.pembrokepublishers.com

Distributed in the U.S. by Stenhouse Publishers
480 Congress Street
Portland, ME 04101-3400
www.stenhouse.com

We acknowledge the financial support of the Government of Canada through the Book Publishing Industry Development Program (BPIDP) for our publishing activities.

We acknowledge the assistance of the OMDC Book Fund, an initiative of the Ontario Media Development Corporation.

Library and Archives Canada Cataloguing in Publication

Brownlie, Faye
    Student diversity : Classroom strategies to meet the learning needs of all students / Faye Brownlie, Catherine Feniak, Leyton Schnellert. — 2nd ed.

Includes bibliographical references and index.
ISBN 1-55138-198-2

    1. Inclusive education. I. Feniak, Catherine II. Schnellert, Leyton III. Title.

LC1200.B76 2006   371.9'046   C2005-907191-5

Editor: Kat Mototsune
Cover design: John Zehethofer
Typesetting; Jay Tee Graphics Ltd.

Printed and bound in Canada
9 8 7 6 5 4 3 2 1

Contents

Foreword

You can tell your writing is making a difference when your thinking is influenced by your readers. Since the publication of *Student Diversity* in 1998, Leyton Schnellert, one of our readers, has joined us as an author. Now it is the three of us who share our perspectives on inclusive Grades 4 to 10 classrooms. In addition, Carole Saundry has contributed her voice to chapter 11—Math: Reaching all learners in the math classroom. We are confident that you will benefit from their contribution to this edition of *Student Diversity*.

We continue to be struck by the power of classroom learning communities that include all learners. When educators strive to let all of their students know that they are competent readers and writers, scientists and mathematicians—that they are competent thinkers—the tone is set for us to learn from one another. The unique perspectives of our students enable us all to learn in new and surprising ways.

Today's classroom continues to be diverse. More than ever, teachers need to be planning inclusive lessons that can celebrate and extend the learning of all. In this second edition of *Student Diversity,* we share how our thinking has unfolded through collaborations with one other, with our teaching partners, and with inspiration from our students.

Putting ideas down on paper requires so many more people than the authors listed on the cover. Our thanks are especially extended to teachers who worked side-by-side with us in their classrooms, helping us refine our practice to include more students. They include Rick Hikida, Cesca Juhasz, Chris Loat, Liz Nasu, Tina Pali, Linda Watson, Fred Weil, Jan Wells, Andrea Western, and Nicole Widdess. To those teachers, administrators, and students too many to mention; from our schools, our workshops, and our university courses; who question, reflect, and learn with us and so sharpen our thinking—thank you!

Our journey toward creating inclusive classrooms where children belong and learn began in 1980, when Faye had the great fortune to meet Susan Close and Linda Wingren in the Young Writer's Project. This was the beginning of a personal and professional relationship that continues to strengthen our lives and our work with children. In the late 1980s, Judith King and Randy Cranston, special educators extraordinaire, pushed us to match our language to our values, to walk the talk for all students. Vicki McCarthy, in the late 1990s, helped us extend to include the ESL learner. We hope that your learning community is filled with educators like these, who expand your thinking.

We believe that teaching is important work. Our classrooms of today are the building blocks of tomorrow's society. We want our society to include everyone in a respectful, honoring way, supporting everyone in being the best they can be. We hope that by entering a conversation with us in our classrooms, you can join with us in constructing learning communities where all lives are enriched by learning and working together—where we discover, in the widest sense of the word, that together we are better.

Faye Brownlie
Catherine Feniak
Leyton Schnellert

Introduction

We believe that teachers need to share the contents of their teaching toolboxes and how they use their tools successfully.

The headlines in our weekend paper scream "Who Are We Calling Special?" In the lead article, the President of the Provincial Intermediate Teachers' Association is quoted as saying "We don't have time and we don't have the tools" to address the learning needs of all the students in the class, including those in the "grey area," who are unidentified but need support. These comments are timely. It is comments like these that propelled us to put our ideas on paper, to write this edition of *Student Diversity*. We believe that it is time to work differently in our schools, in order to better meet the needs of a diverse group of students. We believe that tools do exist for teaching all students, but that they are not necessarily the tools we have been traditionally using. We believe that teachers need to share the contents of their respective toolboxes and how they use their tools successfully, alone and together.

In the past, as resource teachers, our task was to work with select groups of students—to assess their learning, to teach them specific skills, to catch them up, to teach them differently, to give them more individual attention and time. In this role, we were very much captains of our own ships, running our programs and occasionally consulting with teachers as to how they could best support our students when they were in the other teachers' classrooms. We often saw significant progress with our students, particularly when they were in a supported learning situation; i.e., learning with us in a small group. Unfortunately we also heard the comment, "He may do that with you, but in the classroom with everyone else...." We often wished we could have more time with these students in order to really make a difference.

We also have had the opportunity to work more collaboratively as resource teachers, where the expectation is to support the classroom teacher and the class—the diverse class including all students. In this role, we work together with the classroom teacher, pooling our expertise and our resources. We assess the students using provincial performance standards to see what they can do and what they need to be able to do. We use this assessment to design lessons and units that move the students toward accomplishing curriculum goals. We sometimes work side-by-side with the classroom teacher, in the classroom, focusing on how best to support the learning of all students in the context of the ongoing learning expectations. We find our collaboration increases the amount of learning time for students and increases everyone's skill set—our toolbox.

As classroom teachers, we know the weight of responsibility of trying to teach classrooms of diverse students, sometimes feeling that it is just too much, that what we have always done is no longer working. But we also know that there are classrooms where learning *is* happening for all students. We know that books, workshops, and online presentations are available to take us beyond the confines of our personal experiences. We know that when we work as a team in a school we *can* make a difference to student learning, we *can* improve our competencies, and we *can* leave at the end of the day, confident not only that our students feel like they belong in our class but that they—and we—have evidence that they are progressing along their respective learning journeys.

Building Vibrant Learning Environments

Current brain research and learning theory support what intuitive teachers have long known:

- Students need to be actively engaged in learning.
- Students need to belong to a strong community in the classroom.
- Students need to see themselves as able and capable learners.
- Students need to set personal learning goals.
- Students need to be learning in a variety of ways.
- Students need to be emotionally involved in their learning.
- Students learn at different rates.
- Students need rich, in-depth inquiry.
- Students learn best when the content is connected to the world and to their lives.
- Students need choice and clear expectations.

These are foundation statements for our classrooms, and you will see evidence of them in the classroom scenarios in this book. This book is meant to provide teachers with new tools to enable them to better support all the students in their classes, and with ideas for how to minimize their planning time and increase the learning time for their students.

The scenarios described in *Student Diversity* are situated in combined or multi-age classes from Grades 4/5, 5/6, or 6/7, or in single-grade classes from Grades 6 to 10. All the classes support full inclusion of learners with special needs and a collaborative resource model. Each has been affected by a large influx of learners who are learning English as a second or third language. Teachers in these classes are trying to make sense of a curriculum organized by grade-mandated learning outcomes or expectations, criterion-referenced assessment, provincial performance standards, and current learning theory.

In *Reading Next: A Vision for Action and Research in Middle and High School Literacy* (Biancarosa & Snow, 2004), the authors present an interesting mathematical equation: $15 - 3 = 0$.

They suggest that there are 15 research-based strategies to improve adolescent literacy. They also suggest that none of these strategies will make a difference to student learning unless we incorporate these three vital strategies:

- Professional Development: Teachers cannot do this alone. The needs are constantly changing, the knowns are constantly growing, and we must provide structures to support the learning of all our teachers.
- Ongoing Formative Assessment of Students: To make the greatest difference, we must use our assessment information to inform our instruction.
- Ongoing Summative Assessment of Students and Programs: It is our responsibility to check and see that what we are doing is making a difference.

It is our hope that *Student Diversity* contributes to this discussion. We present to you the best of what we have learned from collaborations with teachers who are using their time and their tools to make a difference to the learning of all their students. You may be in a teaching situation without the benefit of a team or a professional learning community. Perhaps *Student Diversity* will become part of your team. Join us as we attempt to put into practice the best of what we know. Together we can improve learning for all.

When thinking literacy strategies, remember this equation: $15 - 3 = 0$.

1 The Classroom as a Learning Community

Stories: The Past

Imagine a combined Grades 4 and 5 class of 29 students. Of this 29, four are level-one and level-two (just beginning) students for whom English is a second language. Five are identified as level-three ESL; one has a severe behavior disorder and is on medication to assist him in self-control and in monitoring his behavior and reactions; one has behavioral challenges but has not yet been identified as having special needs; and one student has a learning disability in the area of expressive output. Support is available for these students, largely on a pullout basis, from the ESL teacher, the resource teacher for students with severe learning disabilities, and the area counsellor. Another of the students in the class sees the area counsellor weekly in a friendship group. Added to this, the learning-assistance teacher supports students who require short-term intervention.

Each of the professionals who support these "children with special needs" is capable and highly supportive of the students and of the classroom teacher. The end result in the classroom, however, is a constantly revolving door; the teacher is left wondering what is actually happening with all the programming for these students, and what she can do to support their learning in her classroom, where they do spend most of their time. Some days, the whole class is together in the classroom for no more than thirty minutes.

Stories: The Present

Return to the same school two years later, and many of these students are now in a combined Grades 6 and 7 class. The class composition is similar to the earlier set-up, but the school has shifted to a collaborative, non-categorical support model. In this model, the classroom teacher is central, and is involved in the design of how support services will be provided to his students. One resource teacher is assigned to each class, and together the classroom teacher and resource teacher establish a plan of how best to address the learning of all the students in the class, including the students identified with special needs. The time available for the resource person to work with the classroom teacher is equal to the combined times of the former various support teachers.

Each team (resource teacher and classroom teacher) receives two hours of planning time at the beginning of the year to determine their course of action. After that, if more planning time is required, it will be sought out on an "as needed" basis. Some students, especially level-one ESL students, may be pulled out of the classroom for direct instruction from time to time. However, most of the support will occur in the classroom, where both the teachers will work with all of the students on their agreed-upon plan. In this classroom, the class is together for the majority of the day.

The Rationale for Inclusion

Inclusion—enrolling students in age-appropriate, regular classrooms—is the norm in North America. It is based on the following beliefs:

- students belong in the regular classroom
- students learn best when they are valued members of a community
- students with special needs require ongoing effective programming, and
- this programming is best provided when a classroom teacher and a single resource teacher collaborate to better meet diverse needs.

Inclusion affects all teachers, not just the regular classroom teacher. When we speak of a non-categorical model of resource support, we mean that the **one** resource teacher for the class works with the classroom teacher to address the needs of **all** students: students who are learning English as a Second Language, the severely learning challenged, the intellectually challenged, students with severe behavior disorders, the physically and multiply challenged, the culturally diverse, students who have mild to moderate learning disabilities or communication disorders.

In the past, the support model was based on aligning specific students with specific teachers. This often resulted in fragmentation of the classroom, as students came and went to see specialist teachers. These specialist teachers searched for time to collaborate with classroom teachers to plan for and re-inforce the students' specific learning goals when these students were in the regular classroom. Working in a collaborative, non-categorical resource model does not preclude one-on-one time outside the classroom for specific students, nor occasional pull-out programs. However, the main focus is providing more effective programming for all students for as much time as possible each day.

We are trying to create a community within the classroom to support learning. All students, including students identified as having special needs, are the responsibility of the classroom teacher. It is critical that we reduce the number of contacts the classroom teacher has with people whose job it is to support the learning of identified students. Too much fragmentation does not support maintaining a vibrant, cohesive learning community.

The Non-categorical Model

Elementary

In our preferred model of support—non-categorical—the roles of the support teachers are amalgamated into a resource support team. A classroom teacher is assigned one non-categorical resource person for a number of periods per week, based on need. The resource teacher works with several classroom teachers, but not the entire school staff. Together the two teachers work out a plan to support the learning of all the students in the classroom including those identified with special needs. The support provided by the resource teacher can occur either inside or outside the classroom, but the plan for support is a collaboration of the two professionals, and is curriculum based. Appropriate adaptations and modifications for learners are tied to learners' needs and to grade-level expectations or learning outcomes.

The spillover from non-categorical support affects many more students than in the traditional support model, including students who are not identified for an Individual Education Plan (IEP), but would benefit from additional teacher time and expertise.

The resource teachers meet as a resource team weekly to consult with one another. This team may include an ESL teacher, a teacher of the learning disabled, a learning-assistance teacher, a teacher with a specialty in autism or behavior disorders. In their daily work, they assist all students. In their weekly meetings, they share their expertise and help one another solve the ongoing challenges in the classes in which they work. Bringing one's special skills to the table enhances the capacity of all involved. The resource teachers are the link to outside support teams (speech and language clinicians, school psychologists, counsellors, district-level special-education consultants, etc.), leaving the classroom teacher freer to concentrate on designing effective learning sequences within the classroom.

Secondary

In secondary schools, the benefits of decreasing the number of support teachers involved with students and teachers are many. In middle and secondary school, students and teachers often struggle to see the whole picture—classes are taught by several different teachers and students do not realize that they can or should use the same effective learning strategies in multiple settings.

Many schools have had significant success when a single resource teacher aligns with a single grade and cross-curricular team of teachers. When a team chooses key strategies and skills to target across a grade, the resource teacher can assist them in modeling these strategies, adapting them across subject areas, and in assisting the team to make units of study more accessible for all students. By introducing supports that address an individual student's learning needs but benefit all students—e.g., text sets, visual support, highlighting key routines, matching selection of teaching strategies to learning outcomes—many more students benefit. Often, resource teachers co-teach in all the classrooms, helping introduce and reinforce key strategies, supports, and routines from class to class. Everyone in the school community benefits and the resource teacher is seen as a valuable and integral member of the team.

Many middle and secondary resource teachers who embrace this model have shared how classroom teachers better understand the many aspects of their work and have built stronger relationships with colleagues. All the students who receive support benefit through access to the core curriculum in the context of the regular classroom. They are given an opportunity to experience success the first time they encounter the content, instead of waiting for a chance to be retaught in the resource room. Most importantly, classroom teachers have benefited from the opportunity to see and experience previously recommended adaptations in action.

Viewpoints

Classroom Teacher

Many schools have had significant success when a single resource teacher aligns with a single grade or team of students.

A change in service delivery model affects each member of the learning community differently.

- Less time is needed to meet with support teachers to plan for, coordinate, and reinforce programming for students with special needs. Because both teachers are together in the room, the question "What did you do with my kids today?" is self-evident.

- With collaborative planning, adaptations and modifications to the ongoing program in the classroom for students with special needs is easier.
- Building a classroom community where all students belong and learn together is possible.
- The expertise of the resource teacher is more available for the classroom teacher and her learning.
- Delivery of the curriculum becomes more differentiated.
- The second set of eyes provided by the resource teacher gives the classroom teacher feedback on the effectiveness of her instruction and where student learning breaks down.
- Support is instantaneous for more students when the second teacher is in the classroom.
- The saying "Two heads are better than one" holds true. The collaboration not only provides more direct service to students, but the emphasis on sharing and the opportunity for sharing expertise is central. This is a professional learning community in action.
- All members of the classroom have a better idea of the purpose of classroom activities and their goal.

Resource Teacher

- The non-categorical model needs only a short startup time. Direct service to students can begin almost immediately, instead of having inordinate amounts of time spent in time-tabling, assessment, individualized (separate) planning, and trying to consult and collaborate with teachers after class.
- Rather than teaching concepts or skills separate from the curriculum, the resource teacher has the opportunity to work alongside an experienced curriculum specialist, to co-plan how best to adapt expectations for the learners with special needs.
- The specialized programming that used to occur in the resource room, which needed reinforcement in the classroom to really benefit the student, is now easier because both teachers can observe each other work.
- The resource teacher gains an understanding of the curriculum expectations of the students, and can use his/her expertise to support students' developing skills, rather than working with a remedial model of learning.
- Weekly resource team meetings provide a trusting environment for asking questions and sharing expertise.
- The focus is on service delivery. There is a shift from concern with labeling to increased concern with addressing the learning needs of students.
- There are fewer classroom teachers to consult with and the consultation is less on "what we did and what you need to do" and more on "what we can do together."
- The expertise and skill of the resource teacher is not reserved for labeled students; most students can benefit from more extensive strategic repertoires.

Students

- Programming for the students who are most at-risk in learning is more consistent.
- Adaptations and modifications are more suitable and immediate for students with significant needs.
- Support is seamless, so intermediate and middle-years students need not suffer the indignation of being removed from their peer group for extra help.
- Feedback on performance toward the learning outcomes of the curriculum is faster. Student performance improves with appropriate, immediate feedback, followed by a chance to practise, both with a coach and independently.
- Identifying students in need of support is a less-arduous task. With two teachers present at key times, support is more readily available and the referral process becomes almost nonexistent. Students do not need to wait to be tested for identification before receiving service.

Parents

- There are no mixed messages. The support person and the classroom teacher align their goals for the student when engaged in continuous, ongoing, side-by-side teaching.
- There are fewer people to talk to after reporting and in IEP meetings. Less intimidation for the family follows from fewer required meetings of the full team with the family.
- The classroom teacher—or possibly the support teacher—will become the primary contact for the parent. This keeps the system from overwhelming the parent with contacts.
- Student learning is enhanced.
- Their children will not only attend a regular school and a regular class, but will belong in it.

Further information about how to establish a non-categorical resource team in your school is available in *Learning in Safe Schools* (Brownlie & King, 2000).

The teaching scenarios in this book have occurred in schools that embrace the non-categorical model of support delivery. You will notice as you read that there are times when two teachers are working together in the class, and other times when the classroom teacher is alone with the students. Most of the service to students with special needs is delivered within the classroom. Rarely are students removed from the class for support. When they are removed, however, the learning expectations and the program have been co-planned by the teacher and the resource teacher, and the alternative setting has been deemed to be more beneficial to the student's learning.

First-Week Considerations

During the first week with a new class of students, we set the tone for the year by involving them in a variety of structured activities that require them to

- meet others in the room
- engage in discussion
- share their findings when reporting back to class

The classroom must be a safe place for everyone if it is to become a community where all students belong.

- reflect on their learning and on their participation
- question
- process new information in different ways
- experience learning as an opportunity for connecting, processing, and transforming and personalizing new information

One of the few rules of the classroom that we officially share with the students is that the classroom must be a safe place for everyone. Students will not take risks in sharing their ideas and fully participating in activities if they perceive that others criticize their opinions. They also do not want to engage in group activities if they feel that they are not welcome to join a particular group. It is critical for our classroom to become a community where all students belong.

During the first or second class, the students are placed in working groups. This can be done randomly or by taking into account the students' requests.

Initially, the students are placed into working groups. If many students in the class know each other already, we have them write down the names of two classmates with whom they would like a chance to work. Using these lists, we try to work in some of the requests each time we make class groupings. Students are guaranteed that, at some point in the year, they will get their first and second choices of groupmates.

Much useful information is gained from this quick sociogram:

- We notice which students are willing to work with any members of the class. These are often students who may be empathetic to all students, including those with special educational needs. We do not want empathetic students exclusively in groups with students with special needs (or vice versa), but at the beginning of the year they can, with only a little support and coaching, be peer models of inclusion for the rest of the class.
- We take note of which students are most and least frequently listed in the student requests. Many times students want the opportunity to work with another student who is not usually in their social group but who is perceived to be academically strong. These students, who look beyond their immediate social group for working partners, are the ones we want to enlist as peer models in the development of social skills.
- The students whose names appear infrequently are carefully placed in groups. We circulate throughout the class during group work, assisting students in the inclusion of all members of the group, in cooperative ways of speaking to each other, and in ways of resolving conflict.

We truly believe in the social aspect of learning and in the students' strong desire to belong. Our personal goal for group work is that, by the end of the year, each student in the class can work with any other student in the class, in a way that promotes the learning of all members of the group.

Day One: A People Search

Participating in this People Search on the first day alerts the students to the fact that this is a class where talking is expected. As we listen to the noise and notice their smiles, we are reminded of what on-task, engaged, happy students look and sound like. We hope to keep this in mind throughout the year.

Having students make lists of preferred groupmates, of course, does not work if most of the students are new to one other; for example, students entering a new, large middle or secondary school from a variety of elementary feeder schools. If this is the case, we proceed to a People Search (Fogarty, 1990) to help students learn their classmates' names and begin to become acquainted.

During the first week, we want activities that will require students to move about the room and speak to each other. In a People Search, students must ask

People Search

Have each person sign in only once! Find someone who, over the summer…

• played a lot of video games _____ _____ Signature	• went overseas _____ _____ Signature
• traveled by train or by boat _____ _____ Signature	• learned how to do something new _____ _____ Signature
• enjoyed spending time alone _____ _____ Signature	• read a great book _____ _____ Signature
• went somewhere they had never been before _____ _____ Signature	• camped _____ _____ Signature
• _____ _____ Signature	• _____ _____ Signature
• _____ _____ Signature	• _____ _____ Signature

See also People Hunt on pages 111 and 112.

their classmates a series of questions in order to discover some of the things that were done over the summer holiday (see People Search, page 15). In this way, every member of the class is approached by others and every member must initiate some conversations. The students love finding out about each other's summers. Even the students who are learning English as a second or third language actively participate in this activity. Once they have heard a question asked, students can use this as a model for approaching others. We move among the students, bridging as necessary to ensure that all are included.

Days Two and Three: A Strategic Sequence

Having now established working groups, we are ready to begin a strategy sequence with a piece of text. There are many different sequences from which to choose. The sequences are built from strategies, each strategy chosen to match a particular purpose:

- **connecting** with background knowledge and with others, building personal questions
- **processing** new information by interacting with it, making new connections, revising former understandings
- **transforming and personalizing** new information so it is stored in long-term memory

We present two different strategy sequences. Both sequences are open-ended enough that all can participate. Both model the active learning we expect in the classroom.

Sequence One: Questioning/Quadrants of a Thought/Information Write

Choose a text. One book we have used is the picture book *A River Ran Wild* by Lynne Cherry, about a river endangered by pollution.

Sequence One consists of these strategies:
1. Questioning (Connecting)
2. Quadrants of a Thought (Processing)
3. Information Write (Transforming and Personalizing)

1. Questioning

- Choose three pictures from the text to share with the students.
- Place the students in groups of four.
- Each group responds to the question, "What do you wonder when you look at this picture?" and records their questions. Students are encouraged to wonder, but to resist the urge to tell or to answer each other's questions.
- Repeat this with each picture, changing the recorder in each group with each picture.
- Ask students to choose their most **creative** question to share from the first picture, their most **thoughtful** from the second, and their most **imaginative** in the third.
- Collect and share these questions from the groups. Try to talk about the questions without answering them. This allows the students to search for personal answers before reading and as they hear the text.
- Discuss the process used in each group to come to consensus on which question to choose. This gives you more information on what social skills to emphasize in the coming weeks.

It is often helpful to have students initially concentrate on two boxes during the reading, and add ideas to the others during the class discussion at each break in the reading.

See chapter 6 for how to use the Quadrants of a Thought strategy to build meaning in a novel study.

2. Quadrants of a Thought

- Have each student fold a piece of paper into four and label the boxes **Image**, **Words**, **Senses**, and **Emotions**.
- Read the text to the students, stopping three times for class discussion, in which students can share what they are filling in on their quadrant sheets.
- As the students share their written and pictorial ideas with each other, encourage them to look for parallels and differences in their thinking.

3. Information Write

- Have a class discussion focusing on what was learned, discovering what surprised the students, and comparing the event in the book to the state of local rivers. (You have begun your year having saved newspaper clippings on pollution in local rivers or other local environmental issues on which people are taking a stand.)
- Students write an information paragraph about what they have learned from the text, from the discussion, and from local news stories.

Sequence Two: Think-Aloud/Visual Thinking/Found Poem

Choose a text. We often use the *Salmon Creek* by Annette LeBox and Karen Reczuch, about the life cycle of the Pacific salmon.

Sequence Two consists of these strategies:
1. Think-Aloud (Connecting)
2. Visual Thinking (Processing)
3. Found Poem (Transforming and Personalizing)

1. Think-Aloud

- Write the first few lines of the text on the board or overhead for all to see. *Salmon Creek* opens with

  > THESE were Sumi's first memories:
  > water over stones,
  > the scent of creek,
  > darkness so complete
  > she could barely imagine
  > another world larger
  > than the egg case enclosing her.

- Read this to the students, explaining what is going on in your mind as you read. For example, you might read, "These are Sumi's first memories:" and say

  > "I wonder who Sumi is? I think this sounds like a girl's name and I guess she owns the memories because of the apostrophe. This makes me wonder about how you can tell a 'first' memory. I don't think mine are from when I was really young. I notice this line ends with a ':' —that usually means a list is coming. I predict the list will be a list of her memories."

- Continue thinking aloud as you read.
- Brainstorm with the students to identify the strategies you used in reading. Write them where the class can see them.
- Write the next piece of text on the overhead. Choose a short piece, as you did with the first excerpt.

- Place the students in partners. One student will read the piece of text aloud to his/her partner, slowing down his/her thinking to show the connections, questions, and ideas he/she has while reading. The partner will coach. The students may choose to use any of the strategies you used, or they may use others.
- Add to the brainstormed list other strategies the students identify.
- Let the partner who was initially the coach now have a turn to do the think-aloud while the other partner coaches. Again, after the discussion, add to the brainstormed strategy list.
- Compliment the students on the depth and breadth of the reading strategies they have. Reinforce that this active reading is what creates long-term memory and what engages readers with text.

2. Visual Thinking

- Have students draw a large thinking bubble on their papers.
- Continue to read the text aloud, not showing the pictures. Have the students draw the images they have in their minds as you read.
- After reading a few pages, stop and collect some of the images that the students are recording.
- Remind students that ideas are meant to be shared in this class and that it is a compliment if someone borrows your idea.
- Continue reading and collecting images for several pages.
- Have students review their images and try to label them with specific language they have heard in the text. It is helpful to model this labeling. Students may wish to label with a partner. The labeling helps them synthesize their thinking about the text, and recall and build specific text language.
- Finish the reading of the text by just reading.

3. Found Poem

- Reread the text the next day, showing the illustrations.
- Read the first quarter of the text again. As you read, have students focus on words or phrases that are so significant that they stay ringing in their ears, even after the text has been read.
- Stop at the end of the first quarter and ask those students whose birthdays are in one quarter of the months of the year to stand (perhaps January, June, and July). Each of these students will contribute a word or phrase. Together, the students will build a poem that captures the essence of this part of the text. Because it is poetry, repetitions are fine, and phrase or sentence length may vary from one word to many. Students are always amazed at how poetic they actually sound and at the many ways these phrases can be ordered to create a different sounding poem.
- Repeat this process, stopping after another quarter of the poem and having another quarter of the birthdays make a poem.
- Continue until all the text has been read and all students have contributed to a found poem. Talk with the students about flow and connections, and about the ease with which they have collaboratively constructed a poem!

- Students, alone or in partners, write a found poem based on their interpretation of the text, their response to the text, a retelling of the text, or whatever you choose your focus for writing to be.

Summary

These initial strategies have been deliberately chosen because they do not require participation solely through print or relying only on individual response. They allow students with special needs to participate, and help those learning English to acquire the language of the curriculum while they are developing their English language. The specific activities have been chosen because we want to emphasize the community that we are building in our classroom and the links that our curriculum will make to the world outside the classroom. We are now ready to delve more deeply into the mandated curriculum and begin our journey together.

All of our students are more able to participate if we allow them talk time, some movement, repetition, small-group work, and opportunities to draw and write their thinking before requiring a written response.

2 Standard Reading Assessment

From Assessment to Instruction

While assessment *of* learning for reporting out is an important purpose, it is not the purpose that most changes student achievement. Assessment *for* learning is.

Assessment serves several purposes. In the past, most assessment was assessment *of* learning, with information collected to use in reporting out progress. Once the information had been collected, the teacher sighed or celebrated, and then moved on.

Assessment *for* Learning

In assessment *for* learning, the primary purpose is to gather information about how students are doing in their learning in order to choose a class focus—to decide what to teach next. The teacher looks for patterns in the students' work, sees what they are able to do and what is missing, and uses this information to design instruction. A series of questions guides these decisions:

1. What can my students do?
2. What is missing?
3. What do I need to teach?

Assessment for learning is a cyclical process. Once the information from the assessment has been gathered, analyzed, and used to design further instruction, teaching continues, fueled by the new information. In four to six weeks, the assessment process is repeated. This return to the assessment allows the teacher to see whether or not the teaching has made a difference, particularly in the focus area. The new results are analyzed, focusing on two new questions:

4. Did my teaching make a difference?
5. If it did, what is my next class goal? If not, what will I do differently in order to assist my students in learning?

Assessment *as* Learning

In assessment *as* learning, the focus is on descriptive feedback.

A third purpose of assessment is assessment *as* learning. In this assessment, the focus is on descriptive feedback. The student is involved in analyzing his/her results and uses this information to set personal learning goals. Thus, each student is aware of and works toward the whole class focus, but also identifies a personal goal. After the first assessment for learning, each student sets a personal goal. After the second assessment, each student poses these questions:

- Did I achieve my goal?
- If not, what else can I do to improve toward this goal?
- If I did, what is my new goal?

This assessment-to-instruction sequence is repeated throughout the school year. Students and teachers work together to explicitly figure out what students can do, what they want to do, how they are going to accomplish this, and finally monitoring their progress toward the curriculum expectations.

Helping Students Assess their Developing Skills

The Standard Reading Assessment is one of the pieces in our assessment file. It is used to monitor students' independent application of the skills and strategies we are teaching in our reading program. These assessments occur regularly, without prior teaching, and are used to keep us and our students informed of their performance and their progress.

In the Standard Reading Assessment, students read and respond to a common text. As the students are completing their response sheets, the teacher or teachers move around the room and listen to each student read a short passage from the text. Students choose which part of the text they will read and have an opportunity to practise it before reading to the teacher. As the student reads, the teacher keeps a modified running record of how the student is reading. This running record is recorded on the student's own text copy and is returned to the student with a compliment about his/her reading, written right on the sheet.

We believe it is important that the classroom teacher and the resource teacher work together on this process whenever possible. Working together, a class of 30 students can be assessed in 45 minutes. Then the two teachers can sit down with the student samples, score them, and together choose a class focus, based on patterns found in the student samples. This process, at first, may take an hour. One of the many benefits of this collaboration is common goal setting. This is particularly important for students at risk, as it provides for them a more consistent program with both teachers reinforcing common goal areas. Initially, the texts we choose for our intermediate students come from *Reading and Responding—Evaluation Resources for Your Classroom* (Jeroski and Brownlie, 2006). These books provide poems, information articles, and narrative text to use for assessment at each grade level. Having a ready supply of good materials is an asset. As we continue with the assessments, however, we find ourselves writing some of the material and choosing other material from classroom texts, brochures, magazines, and newspapers. We usually begin the year using information texts for our assessments. We find that more students are challenged with reading information, so it is critical that we direct our teaching toward this area. In middle and secondary schools, where several teachers share the same group or grade of students, the assessment completed in one class can provide an instructional goal across subject areas.

The response tasks are open-ended, so practise with them supports student learning. Often the response task is kept the same for several assessments while the text changes. The student responses may be drawn, written, or oral, or a combination. This is an assessment of reading, not of writing. By removing the "answer in complete sentences" directive, the focus is on "reading as thinking." There are four different response tasks that we choose from:

1.   i) Using your ideas, images, and feelings, show me you understand.
     ii) What did you notice about your work today?

Our provincial grade-level Performance Standards for Reading describe three aspects of reading: strategies, comprehension, and response or analysis. They describe expected student performance in reading for March/April of the calendar year, on a four-point scale: not yet within expectations, minimally meeting expectations, fully meeting expectations, and exceeding expectations.

We score student samples by highlighting the descriptors in the grade-level Performance Standard that best match the student's work.

We use classroom texts, newspapers, and magazines as texts for our students in Grades 7 to 10.

Practice with common, open-ended responses supports student learning.

2. i) What have you liked or learned in this piece?
   ii) What two questions would you like to ask the author?
   iii) How does what you read connect with what you know?
   iv) What do you think the author wanted you to remember from this text?
   v) What should I notice about your work today?

3. Make notes to show you understand this piece of text. Comment on how you got along with reading and responding.

4. i) Connections: How does what you read connect with what you already knew?
   ii) Summarizing: Choose a way to show the main ideas and details in what you read.
   iii) Inferencing: Read between the lines to find something that you believe to be true, but that isn't actually said. Explain your reasoning.
   iv) Vocabulary: Here are three challenging words from the text. Explain what you think they mean.
   v) Reflecting: Was this easy or hard to understand? How did you help your self understand?

The Assessment Process

1. The teacher reads the title of the passage, sets the stage for the topic or genre of the text. Before beginning to read, the teacher previews the response sheet to help set a purpose for reading. When using the first response—"Using your ideas, images, and feelings, show me you understand"—the teacher brainstorms with the class for what this could look like.

It is important, especially at the beginning of the year, to establish what students think they have permission to do in demonstrating an understanding.

2. A passage and a response sheet are chosen and distributed to each student. The teacher invites the students to read the passage, circling words with which they are unfamiliar.

3. As the students are reading and responding, the teacher moves from student to student and listens to them read. The student chooses a piece of the text that he or she has already practised. The teacher takes the student's piece of text, gives the student a clean copy, and records how well the student reads. The teacher records the following:

omissions ⬯	repetitions h̄om e
substitutions ~~home~~ house	insertions big ᵛ house (old)
reversals of⟩the	don't know (when the word is given to the student) DK
self-corrections S/C	sounds out S/O

Prior to leaving the student, the teacher writes a quick compliment about the reading on the student's page.

Reading for meaning

Their birthday party was such a success that ~~Kayla~~ Karla and Kerry also raised money for the foundation, which carries out the wishes of sick children at their 10th and 11th *birthday* birthday parties. In total, they've raised close to $2,500 ($1,900 US).

4. Once all students have had an opportunity to give an oral reading sample and have completed their responses, all the papers (both the student copy of the text and the student response sheet) are collected for scoring.

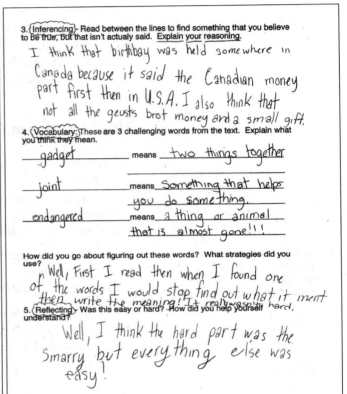

Name: Rachelle _____ Date: _____

Text Title: Parties without Presents

Response Sheet - Intermediate

1. (Connections)- How does what you read, connect with what you already knew? I know that lots of people have so much stuff that on their birthdays they say "You don't have to buy me a present, I already have a lot of things!" That my mom and dad say the exact same thing but they still to it.

2. (Summarizing)- Choose a way to show the main ideas and details in what you read.

Another one said a b-day without presents! / One of the geusts really wanted to pick a present / What geust thought / I guess they really have a good Idea! / No Presents!!! / Parties without presents / 2,500$ (USA 1,900) / I don't get it why wouldn't a kid want presents!!!? / Had B-days joint so more money to raise / They raised 500$ one time then. / raising money / who ever thought of that must be very smart.

3. (Inferencing)- Read between the lines to find something that you believe to be true, but that isn't actualy said. Explain your reasoning. I think that birthbay was held somewhere in Canada because it said the Canadian money part first then in U.S.A. I also think that not all the geusts brot money and a small gift.

4. (Vocabulary): These are 3 challenging words from the text. Explain what you think they mean.

gadget means two things together

joint means Something that helps you do something.

endangered means a thing or animal that is almost gone!!!

How did you go about figuring out these words? What strategies did you use? Well, First I read then when I found one of the words I would stop find out what it ment then write the meaning! It really wasn't hard.

5. (Reflecting)- Was this easy or hard? How did you help yourself understand? Well, I think the hard part was the Smarry but every thing else was easy!

We record the text and date of each assessment on the grade-appropriate Reading Performance Standard (PS). Since this is descriptive scoring, this rubric is not used to assign a number or a rank. The teachers highlight words and phrases on the PS that they have evidence for, based on information that has been observed. The evidence (student text and student response sheet) is stapled to the PS. The BC Performance Standards for reading are available online at www.bced.gov.bc.ca/classroom_assessment/perf.standards

5. All students are included in this assessment. Adaptations are made as necessary for level-one ESL and students with severe reading difficulties. One of the teachers, for example, may work with a small group and read aloud the passage. Sometimes, students are asked to simply read one or two paragraphs, circle the words they know, and draw a picture or diagram of what they believe the passage is about.

6. *Scoring*: Create an overview page for each student for assessments over the year. The text and date of each assessment are recorded on it. Any information that has been observed from the student's oral reading sample, interaction with the student, and the student's response sheet is recorded.

			→	
STRATEGIES	• reads words only; no meaning • dysfluent • waits for help on unfamiliar words • ignores text features	• relies on 1 or 2 specific strategies • careful, halting • uses context clues, if prompted • uses text features, if prompted	• adjusts strategies; reads for understanding • fluent • attempts to determine unfamiliar words • uses text features	• evaluates/ questions own understanding • expressive • independently figures out unfamiliar words • uses text features • effectively
COMPREHENSION	• work is incomplete, inaccurate • does not identify main ideas • unable to make notes • challenged with specific vocabulary	• work is accurate, but lacks detail • identifies most main ideas • makes simple notes with no categories • few inferences • makes some sense of specific vocabulary	• work is clear, detailed, complete • identifies main ideas • makes notes with categories • some inferences • more detailed sense of specific vocabulary	• work is precise and thoughtful • uses own words to express main ideas • makes organized, complete notes • makes inferences • identifies and explains specific vocabulary
ANALYSIS	• unable to connect new information with known	• makes general text to text and text to self connections	• connects new information in several ways	• connects and evaluates new information

(adapted from Grade 5 Quick Scale, *B.C. Reading for Information Performance Standards*)

A different color is used for each assessment. At a glance, teachers, students, and parents can see areas of strengths and weaknesses. Over time, patterns emerge. By reporting period or the end of the year, this sheet has a great deal of information on it about the student's reading performance in independent, text-imposed situations. The information can be read at a glance.

7. *Planning*: Once the class has been scored, the teacher and the resource teacher search for class patterns. What does the class do well? What is a common area of need? Typically we choose one focus from the strategy aspect and one from the comprehension or response aspect. These become our goal areas. These goal areas are shared with the students so everyone knows what we are working toward. As well, as teachers, we decide on two or three specific teaching strategies that we will work on over the next four to six weeks to try to improve student learning in these two goal areas. These strategies are recorded, as shown in the following class example.

	Focus Area	Teaching Strategies
Strategies	• may need help choosing strategies	• daily think-aloud with focus on strategies • daily word-skill modeling and practice (5 min/day), focus on prefixes, suffixes, root words and their connections
Comprehension	• main ideas and details	• collaborative summary • what's important and why • power paragraph

As students gain experience using the PS, they can then share their progress with their parents at student-led conferences.

8. *Sharing.* It is important that the students are also involved in this feedback cycle of assessment. Often, after the first assessment, we do not have individual conferences with students about their performance on the assessment. We share the information about the class's performance as we use student samples to collaboratively build criteria. After the second assessment, when students have had an opportunity to engage in this form of response and have participated in very focused, deliberate teaching, we conference with students, emphasizing their progress toward the specific class focus and helping them set personal goals.

Using the Information

Assessments are worth doing when they give teachers information to inform their practice. We need to see that our teaching is making a difference. The following scenarios are typical of the action taken as a result of information collected on the class assessment.

1. Building Criteria for Powerful Response

When choosing student response samples, try to include a variety of representations—web, paragraph, pictures, etc. Samples are chosen because they are powerful in some way; they have achieved some of the descriptions of more sophisticated reading behavior.

From time to time, the teacher chooses five or six student response samples, makes them into overhead transparencies, and shares them with the class. The samples are shown to the class, one at a time, with the comment, "I have chosen a variety of your responses to use as samples. These samples will help us build criteria for what really works or what is powerful in this type of response." The students are asked, "What strikes you as powerful about this sample?" or "What do you notice that really works in this sample?" The questions are positive, and only positive comments are accepted. These comments are recorded on the chalkboard or on chart paper. Once all the response samples have been reviewed, the teacher and class review their comments and reorganize them into a more coherent form. These are posted to guide other text responses the students might be doing over the next four to six weeks — that is, allowing them to practise the desired behaviors in a variety of supported and independent contexts before being assessed again. This list of criteria is also used by students to self-assess their responses from the assessment and to set a personal reading goal for the next month. These goals will vary greatly from

Prompt: "Using your ideas, images and feelings, show me you understand."

student to student, but each student chooses a goal within the context of the class goals and graded curriculum expectations. Patterns noticed in the class's reading behavior indicate direction for teaching in the next four to six weeks.

In the following samples, Grades 6 and 7 students have responded to an information text "Pollution Blamed for Seal Deaths" (Jeroski and Brownlie, 2006; grade 6). They had been asked: "Using your ideas, images and feelings, show me you understand."

In the criteria-building session, Ronnie's is the first sample. The students notice that Ronnie has shown *cause and effect* (the factories and the toxic wastes in the water) and *emotion* (the seal cub calling out to the mother).

Michelle's is the second sample and the students add *main idea and some good details from the article* and *summary* to the list.

> Pollution Blamed For Seal Deaths   Michelle
>
> Because of pollution, about 7000 harbour seals have died. In West Germans waters, another 2000 have died. This has been one of the worst ever ecological disasters Each year, 400,000 tonnes of oil leak into the ocean. Too much toxic waste are dumped in the ocean. Scientist have found tumors and lesions in fish, caused by the toxic waste.

Finally, Anita's sample is shown. The students notice her *details from the text* and the *relationships* shown on her web.

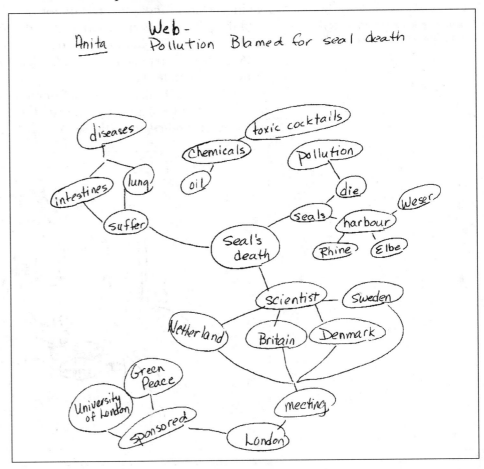

The criteria list that is posted includes the following:

- main idea and some specific details
- emotional connection
- how ideas fit together—their relationship to each other
- extending—thinking beyond the text
- cause and effect
- summary—be sure we can tell you have read the text, not just used your own ideas

2. Small-Group Support

A few days after the assessment, either the classroom teacher or the resource teacher collects the students who had difficulty with reading the text or with a particular response, along with the text that they read, and their responses. During this small-group mini-lesson, teacher and students look at the words circled, discussing how to say these words and possible meanings. Next, they choose a part of the text to read aloud together, discussing as they read, the connections they are making and what they are thinking about. Finally, they

If a small group of students are experiencing difficulty with reading the text or with a particular response, these students can rework the challenging part of the assessment with support.

return to the response. If the students had been asked to respond to more than one question, only one is chosen as a focus during this conference.

The question is read aloud and ways to respond to the question are discussed. When the teacher is confident that this entire group of students is more able to respond to the question, the students retry the question. These responses are marked "with support," scored, and charted with the symbol *WS*, to indicate what the student could do with support. This not only allows the students explicit, direct instruction for the desired achievement, but also boosts their confidence, because they have now witnessed themselves as more able to perform. The teacher has specific information on where the students were experiencing difficulty, and on what strategies were effective in supporting the students. These, then, are applied, as appropriate, in a variety of contexts in the next four to six weeks.

In this sample, notice the change in Christine's response to a prompt from a Grade 5 selection "Flying" (Jeroski and Brownlie, 2006; grade 5): "Using your ideas, feelings, and images, show me in writing that you understand the story."

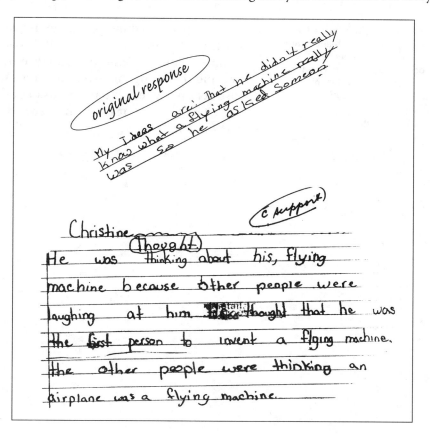

3. Vocabulary

Initially, students who are learning English often have a long list of miscued words. They become very proud of their accomplishments, seeing the list diminish as they acquire English vocabulary.

As we score the responses, miscued words are noted. Individual lists are dated and charted on the student's sheet. These words can be read and talked about in small groups with the resource teacher. Sometimes the students practise these new "hard" words for homework. A class list of miscued words is also kept. In mini-lessons of five to ten minutes over the next two weeks, the teacher returns to these words and studies them with the class. This study includes strategies for decoding the words—such as phonics and structural analysis—and strategies for making sense of the meaning.

4. Preparation for the Next Standard Reading Assessment

At the beginning of the next assessment, the students revisit the criteria developed from the five or six student response samples. This assessment will use a different reading passage, perhaps a different genre of text, or different response questions. To begin the next assessment, the students and teacher review the criteria and decide which of those items listed will be important to consider in this assessment. They may add or delete items. The students are also reminded of their personal reading goal. They are invited to think about the criteria prior to reading, "When you begin to demonstrate your understanding, what will you keep in mind?" Following the assessment, they return to their response and reflect, "What should I notice that you did today?" (referenced to the criteria) and "What will I keep in mind for next month?"

The Standard Reading Assessment is just one part of our classroom assessment program. We aim to administer it five or six times a year, to monitor the changes in our students' performance and to see the impact of our teaching. We find that using this assessment on a regular basis helps us keep our instruction aligned with the needs of our students. This alignment improves our effectiveness as teachers and reminds us to constantly keep our focus on our students.

We find it useful to use the same response questions and the same genre of text at least two or three times in a row. This allows the students to directly apply the skills and strategies that they have been taught, based on the results of the last assessment.

A webcast detailing how to use the Standard Reading Assessment to inform instruction is available online at www.bced.gov.bc.ca. Go to Literacy, then to Webcast, Part 1, Faye Brownlie, Literacy in the Middle Years.

3 Getting Strategic with Strategies

Planning from Assessment Results

From the beginning of the year, we focus on creating learning experiences that help all of our students grow and succeed. For us this means determining which skills our students need to develop while learning about important and often new concepts.

When classroom and resource teachers work together to use and adapt strategies for students in the classroom, it becomes easier to see what aspects of the content students are understanding and which ones they need more experience with. When two teachers plan and work together, there are always more ideas for creating and adapting lessons and strategies to meet the needs of the diverse learners in the classroom. Resource teachers can help classroom teachers choose a strategy or approach that matches the skills a class needs to develop, can help match the strategy to the text or activity that will be used, and can adapt the strategy for students who need more support.

To plan lessons and units, we collect a great deal of information about our students early in the year. As we get to know each student and what is unique and special about them, we strive to build a classroom community that honors and encourages diversity.

Student Learning Portfolios

We use the first term of school to help each student build a learning portfolio. We begin to explore the notion of each student documenting his/her own individual personal history. We also begin with a focus on personal writing (see chapter 5).

Students collect the information from the various sources and put it into their learning portfolios. Teacher Linda Watson helped each student in her Grade 9 class create a summary of what he/she believed to be the most relevant and important information (see sample on page 32). This learning profile became the introductory section to each student's Humanities portfolio. At the end of each term the students updated their learning profiles based on the goals they had set, what they had done to achieve these goals, and any additional information that they had learned about themselves over the term. The portfolio was then handed in as part of their term's assessment. Having students create a personal summary of their learning as the introductory task in their portfolios helped Linda emphasize that reflection and goal setting are a priority in teaching and learning in her classroom.

Building a Class Profile

On the *Getting to Know You* graphic organizer (pages 33 and 34) is a set of questions that we have used in our Grades 4 through 10 classrooms to begin the process of building a class profile. When the front and back of the organizer are reproduced on the two sides of a sheet, the front of the organizer looks at strengths and interests. It asks students to tell us, from their point of view, what we really need to know about them. The back of the graphic organizer looks at fears. *Getting to Know You* is the first step in our assessment cycle for the year. Once we collect this information, we pull it out for every unit we plan.

Together we examine the individual *Getting to Know You* sheets. We use this information about our students to guide our instruction. In Linda's class we decided on three key areas of focus:

1. Students needed to focus their attention on specific content. To do this we built steps into lessons where students could both analyze the tasks they engaged in and determine what the tasks required of them.

2. The group was very active. To capitalize on their energy, we ensured that each phase of our lessons included opportunities for all students to talk, and provided opportunities for students to represent their learning artistically and symbolically.

3. We were reminded to be explicit about key concepts in each lesson, so that we could modify tasks and activities for students who had a difficult time understanding, remembering, and/or applying new or abstract concepts.

Class Profile: Humanities 9 blocks C/D

Dates:	Strengths	Stretches	Interests/ Passions	GOALS
Fall assessment for learning	– outgoing – self-aware – friendly – sense of humor – co-operative – enjoy reading – a positive atmosphere in the class	– risk taking to show their invisible knowledge – showing what they know – focusing, concentration – finding main ideas, details – making connections between what they know and what they read – some students with written output challenges – several students on modified programs	– movement (almost any kind) – cooking – creating things – visual art (some) – drama (some) – sports (some) – socializing	– create a safe classroom – help students understand the phases of teaching and learning – use the connection, processing, transforming phases to support risk-taking, sharing and self-advocacy – focus and reading in SS and writing in ELA during the first term – target making connections and finding the main idea
Winter assessment for/of learning				
Spring assessment for/of learning				

Getting to Know You

All About _____

Words that Describe Me...	My Favorite Books/Stories Are...	Things I Like To Do With My Friends	My Favorite Activities when I'm Alone	My Favorite Activities when I'm with My Family
			Very Favorite: Other Activities:	
I'm Very Interested In or Good At...	Things I'd Like You to Know About Me (or you need to know about me)	My Hopes and Dreams For Myself Are...	The easiest ways for me to show what I know are...	One thing I would like to get better at in school this year

Flip...

N. Widdess, L. Watson & L. Schnellert, 2005

Getting to Know You (back)

Shhhhhhh!!!!
My greatest fears are...

Designing Lessons

Using teaching strategies certainly makes learning new concepts fun, as students are more likely to participate in lessons that include engaging approaches. However, we also want our students to internalize the skills a teaching strategy targets and eventually apply these skills to their independent work. Once the lesson is over and the board has been erased, we want the students' memory of how and why we engaged them in the topic to stay with them. A good lesson is a thing of beauty. When we link strategies and lessons together in a way that introduces students to new concepts and builds their skills over time, learning becomes fun and student performance increases.

We have key learnings from brain research in mind as we begin to design our lessons:

- engage students by tapping into their interests and emotions
- show new information to students in a variety of ways
- provide students with different ways to show what they know (Rose & Meyer, 2002)

With this as the base, we add in our phases of teaching support for students' learning: connecting, processing and transforming/personalizing. By planning with these key learning phases in mind we are able to ensure that we make adaptations for all of our learners in each phase.

Connecting: Connections that Last

Remember the phases of learning:
- Connecting
- Processing
- Transforming/personalizing

Our first hurdle is engaging and motivating students. This phase of teaching and learning is all about connecting. To help students connect to the topic, we ask them to brainstorm what they know about a topic, begin a lesson with a simulation, have students sort and categorize vocabulary words, or pose some intriguing questions. There are many ways to help students get ready for new learning.

Processing: Actively Engaging with New Content

Once we help students activate their prior knowledge and set a purpose for their reading, we focus on developing and applying processing strategies. These strategies help readers construct meaning, compare new knowledge to prior knowledge, and determine what is important. The modeling and practising of these processing strategies teaches students to monitor their understanding while reading (Tovani, 2000; Wilhelm, 2001).

Transforming and Personalizing: Creating Lasting Memories

After successfully making meaning of the text, students are encouraged to demonstrate their understanding. We focus on strategies that keep students generating responses to deepen and personalize their understanding—to commit what they are learning to long-term memory.

Successfully creating powerful learning experiences for our diverse classes has led us to focus on incorporating teaching strategies that help students generate and use their own learning strategies. We help them understand what good readers, writers, and thinkers do, in order to help them become good readers, writers, and thinkers.

We do this in three ways:

- choose one or two key strategies to focus on at a time
- mentor students to acquire these strategies
- once they are familiar with our expectations and we have spent a great deal of time modeling ways to use a strategy, encourage students to create and adapt their own strategies

- Choose your teaching strategies based on the skills you want to target.
- Explain to students how and why the teaching strategies you have chosen will help them.

By choosing just a few teaching strategies each term, we can ensure that students have an opportunity to master both the strategy and the thinking behind it. Our instructional planning becomes easier as we carefully choose a few strategies and weave them across the various subject areas and units of study. While the resource teacher has a few students who may need adaptations and/or modifications, all students can benefit from most recommendations. With a resource teacher and classroom teacher working together, planning lessons that build the same skills for all students, all students learn the same key strategies and then apply them to tasks where they can have success.

Starting with Information Text

In chapter 7, you will read how teacher Nicole Widdess moved from fiction to non-fiction in her slavery themed unit. In Linda Watson's class, students started with non-fiction and moved into fiction.

As students move from grade to grade and from elementary to secondary school, they have to read more and more informational text. By Grade 10, seven out of a student's eight classes require him/her to work with a specialized type of text that is unique to that subject area. With this in mind, we want to build awareness, confidence, and the skill sets of our students. Even before our initial assessment, we begin by setting up routines and a common lesson structure in our classes.

Choosing Strategies to Teach

We deliberately explain to the students that each lesson has a connecting, processing, and transforming/personalizing stage, and that each phase asks a reader to do different things. We often use the following questions to help us target specific skills in each lesson.

- Connecting: How will I help my students get ready for new material?
- Processing: How will I help my students monitor their reading/learning?
- Transforming/Personalizing: How will I help my students use and integrate new information?

As we plan our lessons, we further refine our strategy focus by completing sentence stems for each phase.

Connecting: How will I help my students get ready for new material?

To help them

- set a purpose for reading/learning, I'll…
- activate prior knowledge, I'll…
- survey the text, I'll…
- set reading goals, I'll…

Processing: How will I help my students monitor their reading/learning?

To help them

- narrow their focus, I'll…
- maintain their attention, I'll…
- be accountable for their thinking, I'll…
- identify important ideas, I'll…
- compare new knowledge to prior knowledge, I'll…
- ask questions, I'll…
- summarize or paraphrase, I'll…

Transforming/Personalizing: How will I help my students use and integrate new information?

To help them

- demonstrate understanding in a variety of ways, I'll…
- organize information to remember it, I'll…
- identify what they still need to learn, I'll…
- put ideas into their own words, I'll…

The strategies chosen are purposeful. It is using these purposeful strategies that we model in our think-alouds.

We have found that in the fall students often ask us which phase of the lesson we are in; by Christmas students begin to name the phase of the lesson. If a lesson spans two or more classes, our students begin the class by reminding us which phase we were in the previous day. At the end of the year, we find it extremely gratifying to have students tell us which strategies they found most helpful and effective. We have found a wide range in students' preferred strategies. As a result, we build in opportunities for students to choose the strategy they would use, alter it, and/or create their own.

Planning with Reading Skills in Mind

In our teaching, we use our Standard Reading Assessment (chapter 2) results to choose and plan our strategy focus for each term.

For Linda's Humanities 9 classes, we chose to focus on determining importance when reading non-fiction, as both of her classes struggled in this area on the Standard Reading Assessment. We decided that orienting the students to the textbook and introducing them to key concepts related to the big idea of Change would be a perfect opportunity to practise these skills. As we planned each lesson, we had to decide what the essential concepts were, what reading skill(s) we were targeting, and what teaching strategies we would use to connect, process, and transform/personalize (see Humanities 9 Planning chart on page 39, and Lesson Planning template on page 38).

We tried to select key strategies to use several times over the course of the term and year. We've put a star beside these strategies in the planning chart. Our intention, in choosing and targeting certain strategies over the course of the year, is for students to have an opportunity to practise these skills with different texts, themes, and concepts while building their understanding of how a strategy helps them.

Lesson Planning

Lesson:

Big Ideas of today's lesson (Key concepts/essential understandings):
Students will understand that…

Student outcomes (important skills or processes):
Students will be able to…

Connecting	**Purpose:** Engagement/Activate prior knowledge/Predict content/ Focus on a purpose for reading **I will…**	**What I'm thinking:** How can I tap into my students' interests, offer appropriate challenges, and increase motivation?
Processing	**Purpose:** Construct meaning/ Monitor understanding/Process ideas **I will…**	How will I help my students interact with new ideas that they encounter?
Transforming/ Personalizing	**Purpose:** Process ideas/Apply knowledge/Reflect on thinking and learning **I will…**	How can I provide learners alternatives for demonstrating what they know?

Assessment
If students are engaged and I have modeled this well, I hope that they will:

1.   2.

3.   4.

Year Planning

We begin our planning by identifying engaging themes and units that cut across subject areas. In planning Linda's Humanities 9 unit, we looked for the big ideas and key concepts in social studies and examined how these might fit with their English Language Arts (ELA) program. We were able to determine one big idea for the year for Social Studies: Revolution Leads to Change. Then we looked at the learning outcomes for social studies and ELA. It was not hard to plot these into the overall plan. We created a separate box on our planning template for our reading skill target, to keep it in mind at all times. As we planned our lessons, considering the connecting, processing, and transforming/personalizing phases, we found ourselves choosing a variety of teaching strategies that could help us get at that reading skill. We were not able to be too firm in our choice of skills and strategies, because we did not know how quickly the students would progress. This chart records what we did.

Humanities 9 Planning Chart
Big Ideas: Change, Power, Making a Difference

	Sept 13 - Oct 12	Mid October	November	December
ELA ESSENTIAL LEARNING OUTCOMES	(1) use language creatively to explore & express thoughts/ideas/feelings experiences (2) work individually and in small groups and as a class to explore ideas, accomplish goals, maintain relationships and build community	(1), (2), (3) (4) appreciate the power and beauty of language in their own creations and others (5) use rubrics and examples to assess own writing and language development	(1), (2), (3), (4), (5), (6) respond creatively, personally and analytically in written, spoken, and graphic form to a variety of poetry, fiction and non-fiction language (7) apply knowledge and conventions of language in their written and spoken expression	(1), (2), (3), (4), (5), (6), (7), (8) generate a focused research topic, then gather , organize information for a variety of writing tasks (9) use language analytically to form, express, defend an opinion on a controversial issue
ENGLISH LANGUAGE ARTS	**Change theme** Writer's Workshop: Memoirs **Activities:** All About Me... What is Powerful Writing Writing our Basic Story Modeling Memoir Writing Cracking Open Your Memoir Commonplace books*	**Change theme** Writer's Workshop: Poetry **Activities:** Heart Mapping (Atwell) Where Poetry Hides (Atwell) Metaphors Similes Personification	**Heroes and Icons Theme** Reading Focus: Modeling *Introducing a new reading strategy using poem* **Activities:** What do good readers do? Think Alouds Poetry -Making Connections -Goal Setting -Author's message Partner talk	**Breaking Through Labels Theme** From read aloud to Literature circles with same novel • Iqbal, Francesco D'Adamo *Introducing a new reading strategy using picture book* **Activities** Imaging 4 Quadrants Asking Questions Big Talk (small grp) Big Talk Guidelines Creating an image/symbol Quickwrite
SOCIALS ESSENTIAL LEARNING OUTCOMES	(1) describe and assess the factors influencing the development of identity and the roots of social and cultural issues (2) gather, interpret and evaluate information *ELA #3 develop and apply extensive strategies to anticipate, predict & confirm meaning*	(1), (2), (3) examine the contributions of the French Revolution to the development of democratic concepts (4) define conflict and revolution	(1), (2), (4), (5) identify and clarify a problem, issue or inquiry (6) examine a variety of perspectives and defend a position on a controversial topic (7) define colonialism, imperialism, nationalism	(1), (2), (4), (5), (6), (7) assess how economic systems contributed to the development of early Canada (8) plan, revise, document, defend and present information
SOCIAL STUDIES	Change Comes to Europe • Modern Age, Fight for Democracy. English Civil War **Strategies:** Think alouds: Seeing reading Think/Pair/Share* Skimming and scanning Mind mapping* Writing in role Who are the Players* Chunking text* Finding and Using the Back Story	French Revolution **Strategies:** Critical timeline* Think/Pair/Share* What's important & Why* Who are the Players* Mind mapping* 3 Sticky Notes = 3 ideas Image/Icon Two column notes*	Napoleonic Era **Strategies:** What's Important & Why* Two Column Journal* Acting out a Player Critical Timeline* Reciprocal Teaching (Palinscar) Think/Pair/Share* Tableau	Industrial Revolution "The Nature of Work" **Strategies:** Think/Pair/Share* Two column journal* Make a prediction Think aloud What's important & Why What's Fair (importance) Most important and why
READING SKILLS	Determining Importance	Determining Importance	Determining Importance, Prediction & Making Connections	Determining Importance, Asking Questions & Imaging

Introducing a New Strategy

Initially we introduce a class to a new strategy by explaining that we have chosen our focus based on the results of the Standard Reading Assessment; we explain how the strategy works.

When we introduce a new reading skill that we want to focus on, we first model what the strategy looks like using a think-aloud. Over the next week or so, students get several opportunities to try the skill out in the fiction and non-fiction texts in our thematic units. We chunk the text into smaller pieces so we can stop and explain our thinking. This helps both teachers and students be explicit about what they are doing.

To introduce the first reading strategy, we model the strategy with a think-aloud. A copy of the text has been made into an overhead and, with the text on the overhead and pen in hand, we share what we are thinking and record it on the overhead. The following sequence is a sample of the lessons taught in Linda's classroom.

Change and the Industrial Revolution

Purpose: Engagement/Activate prior knowledge/Predict content/Focus on a purpose for reading:

Strategy: Think/Pair/Share

1. "Think of an invention or form of technology that has changed the way you live your life."
2. In partners, students discuss examples as the teacher moves around the class, supporting as needed.
3. Create T-chart on the board: Big Changes in 21st/22nd century and Big Changes from 1700 on.
4. Have groups discuss their inventions. List on the board. Draw out what the big change was and put in chart.

Purpose: Identify possible changes/Support answers

Strategy: 3 Sticky Notes = 3 changes

1. Read first chunk from the text out loud; put sticky note by a possible change.
2. Discuss your choice with the class.
3. Students place sticky notes and share with a partner.
4. Present two more chunks of information and have students read to identify two more changes, placing their sticky notes by them.
5. Debrief as a class. Fill in chart together.

Purpose: Process Ideas/Reflect on Thinking and Learning

Strategy: Quick Write

1. Review criteria for quick writes.
2. "Using what we've just read – what do you think the Industrial Revolution is all about?"
3. "Make a prediction using webs, words, pictures, charts, etc. Show me your best thinking."

Over time we move from teacher modeling and the guiding of student skill use to collaborative use of the strategy in texts of students' own choice. We use literature and information circles as opportunities to apply key reading skills in a real-world manner.

Linda moved from modeling to partner work to literature circles over several months. There had been ample practice of comprehension skills and strategies during reading activities in the fall. In the winter, the students came prepared for their conversation, knowing what strategy they needed to focus on. With a few key ideas and responses in mind, students used the Say Something strategy (see chapter 7) to start their conversations.

The year plan on page 41 is an example of what teachers can do to teach the skills of content-area reading while building students' reading skills. Linda was able to identify the main concepts and themes that she wanted her students to explore and then built her year around these ideas. Once these big ideas were identified, it was easy to plan out lessons that helped students build their skills while exploring a concept or theme that lasted over the course of a unit of study. By using the results of the Standard Reading Assessment, Linda was able to choose a skill to focus on for a month to six weeks. She saw students become more proficient in this skill because they had time to master it.

Linda moved from modeling a strategy with one text to introducing collaborative literature circle conversations, through independent application with students' own literature book choices.

Literature Circles
Topic: The industrial revolution and child slavery
Big Ideas: Change, Making Connections

	Lesson 1 Focus: Making connections	Lesson 2 Focus: Making connections	Lesson 3 Focus: Collecting info for conversations	Lesson 4-10 Focus: Making images in your mind
Connecting	**Read aloud:** *Iqbal* ➤ Moving into literature circles with a common novel -Read chapter one of *Iqbal* -Make predictions and connections using the title and cover -Share predictions and questions with a partner and then the class	**Read aloud:** *Iqbal* -Discuss important connections homework to refresh memory of chapter one -remind students that focus is on text:text, text:self and text:world connections -revisit the book talk criteria	**Read aloud:** *Aunt Harriet's Underground Railroad in the Sky* ➤ Introducing a new strategy -set purpose of collecting ideas for literature circle conversations -using the first page of the story, model the collection of images and descriptive/powerful language	**Read aloud:** Continue use of 4 Quadrants and group conversations with *Iqbal*
Processing	Read aloud chapter and stop 3 times to allow students to jot connections down in their logs	Read aloud chapter 2 and stop 3 times to allow students to jot connections down in their logs	-Ask students to do the same from second page -Look for example that students could add to the 4 Quadrants on the overhead -repeat with next two pgs -model one emotion -repeat and add wonder	**Explore using** -Sticky notes -Double-entry journals -Listen, Sketch and Draft
Transforming/ Personalizing	-Share connections in small groups -Generate criteria – what makes a good book conversation	New groups of 4 – book conversations Revise the criteria in small groups, students assess selves: one strength, one goal for next time	-Finish up book with asking student to add to quadrants that need more examples -exit slip	Using illustrations from picture books to introduce questioning
Homework	• *Quick write – explain 3 important connections that you made*	• *Quick write – explain 3 important connections that you made*	• N/A	*Targeted reflections, ie. explain which images were most powerful and why*

	Lessons 11-15 Focus: Making connections	Lesson 16 Focus: Making connections	Epilogue Focus: Comprehension activity	Moving into new books Focus: Making images in your mind
Connecting	**Read aloud:** *Iqbal* -Book talks – introduce students to the industrial revolution literature circles titles • *Midnight is a Place* • *The Grave* • *Street Child* • *Crispin* • *Oliver Twist* Listen, Sketch, Draft is a chance to show what you can do – make sure you have all 4 parts of the quad and your connections	**Read aloud** Have students decide on top three books for industrial revolution Brainstorm as a group what else can be added to the discussion criteria	**Read aloud:** *Iqbal* Focus on creating an image that represents Iqbal (relate to the symbol work done in Social Studies). You may wish to represent Iqbal as a symbol of the battle again child slavery and/or violence	**Send into new groups based on book choice** **Explain use of** -Sticky notes -Double-entry journals -Listen, Sketch and Draft Evaluation will be based on discussion and responses
Processing	Read aloud chapter and stop 3 times to allow students to jot images, words, wonders and feelings down	Read aloud chapter 15 -student choice for "note-taking"	-Ask students to listen for details to support the development of their symbol	Say Something strategy
Transforming/ Personalizing	-Book groups -How does hearing about others' images change your thinking?	Book discussion groups Students assess themselves: one strength as a group, one goal for next time	Criteria: -you can use any media in your work -must relate to feelings and emotions -make the viewer wonder -must have combination of images or one detailed icon/symbol	Group assessment
Homework	*How does hearing about others' images change your thinking?*	*Quick write – what did you notice in this chapter? How did you represent your thinking? Why?*	*Work on image*	*Two-column journal*

Summary

Perhaps you would be more comfortable starting by co-planning a single lesson sequence. Using the Lesson Planning template on page 38, you can work with a teaching partner to create a lesson that has connecting, processing, and transforming/personalizing phases in it. Targeting a key skill over several weeks leads to increased success for all class members.

Many teachers find collaboratively planning units with their resource teachers to be an immense support. In co-planning units, two teachers can better address student diversity and support and extend the learning of all students. Co-planning content, structure, and strategy creates engaging learning opportunities for all. The classroom teacher brings her curriculum content expertise and knowledge of the key concepts required to understand the subject. The resource teacher contributes a background in reading skills and strategies and supporting students at risk. Together, this is a winning team.

4   Writers Workshop: The Foundation

We believe that Writers Workshop is the model that best supports students' development as writers.

Our writing program is the unifying factor that links to all that we do in the classroom. It has changed the way we think about planning for teaching, and this has affected the way the students view themselves as learners. It is both powerful and inclusive, as the students' written compositions attest.

In order for students to become skilled writers, they need explicit teaching and lots of time to practise and develop their writing skills. Writers Workshop incorporates writing instruction, extended time for writing, student choice, and student collaboration. The structure of the workshop differentiates for all students as they set personal learning goals while working as part of the classroom community within a whole-class focus. Finally, assessment information is part of the workshop conversation, linking instruction and learning. Students from Kindergarten through secondary can participate in the Writers Workshop. It begins with a simple idea: everyone has a story to tell. The sharing of these stories helps build a classroom learning community. With these stories as a basis, the instructional focus is determined and students develop their skills as authors.

Establishing an Environment for Authors

We were profoundly influenced by the early work of Donald Graves and his colleagues, such as Nancie Atwell. Initially it was Atwell's *In the Middle* (1998) that helped us set our course. More recently we have been influenced by *Lessons That Change Writers* (2002).

Atwell (1998) outlined some guiding principles to consider when setting up a Writers Workshop:

- Regular time must be devoted to writing.
- Authors should have the opportunity to choose their own topics.
- Authors need feedback specific to their writing.
- Authors learn the mechanics of writing in the context of their compositions.
- Authors should have time to discuss their writing and read the work of other authors.
- Authors need to read widely.
- Teachers should be knowledgeable about current trends in writing instruction.

We have added on several of our own:

- Authors benefit from teacher modeling.
- Authors sometimes need specific instruction to follow whole-group lessons.
- Writing improves with the development of, not the assignment of, specific criteria.

The stages of the writing process:
- pre-writing
- drafting
- editing
- proofreading
- presenting and sometimes publishing

These stages are never considered to be linear.

- Personalized goal setting and self-assessment can enhance student interest and motivation.
- All writers can benefit from, and find success in, a workshop environment.

Writers Workshop works best when an extended period of time (at least 80 minutes) is built into the timetable once or twice each week. It is an ideal time for in-class collaborative teaching with the resource teacher. Together the classroom teacher and the resource teacher determine the needs of the range of students and how best to address these needs. When together in the classroom, the two teachers model, conference, and provide feedback for students individually or in small groups, run editing circles, or teach mini-lessons. During the workshop time, students are involved in the various stages of the writing process: pre-writing, drafting, editing, proofreading, presenting, and sometimes publishing. Sometimes these stages occur with all students simultaneously, sometimes not. Never are these stages considered to be linear.

A typical lesson plan for Writers Workshop includes the following activities:

- a mini-lesson taught by the teachers, sometimes as a whole class and sometimes as two smaller groups
- a Status of the Class check to find out the writing topic that each student is currently working on
- quiet time for students to write
- individual or small-group conference time with the teachers
- an opportunity to have a short conference with another author
- group sharing time, when authors read a passage from their writing and the rest of the class listens and provides feedback

Day One: Getting Students Started

On the first day of Writers Workshop, the goal is to get each student writing about a personal experience. A typical prompt is to ask students to visualize some of the places, people, things, and events that they have experienced over the summer holiday. We model each part of the process for the students, then invite them to follow our process and borrow any of our ideas to spark their thinking.

Pre-writing: Finding a Topic

1. Students think of three related topics and record them on paper.

2. The teacher models this process on the blackboard or overhead using everyday topics; e.g., Grandma, amber, and kayaking.

3. Students ask questions of the teacher about the topics. The teacher encourages questions that make connections, add details, and help the writer use expressive language.

4. Students share their three topics with a partner and engage in the same questioning process.

5. Students question each other to learn more about the topics.

Pre-writing: Going Deeper with the Topic

1. Each student begins to record a web of ideas for any or all of the three topics.

   • ESL students show their thinking in a web using drawings and words.

2. From their webs, students each choose one topic to write about.

3. Partners interview each other using open-ended questions to prompt each other to discuss ideas not yet included in the web.

4. Final details are added to the web after this interview.

Drafting

1. As students are ready, they move from their web to writing a first draft of their story. The teachers also write.

2. After ten minutes of writing, one of the teachers moves through the room to support students as required.

3. Students write for 15–20 minutes.

Editing and Sharing

1. Each writer in the class, including the teacher, reads aloud his/her first sentence, the lead.

2. The class identifies what catches their attention or what works in the leads. Frequently, students will notice that effective leads are humorous, use dialogue, or use action to gain attention

3. These ideas are recorded. They will be used in a later mini-lesson on leads.

4. The teacher reinforces how much the students already know about leads. This has been the first mini-lesson.

A lead is defined as a sentence that introduces the writing topic and helps to establish the writer's voice. It captures the reader's attention early in the writing.

Day Two: Editing and Building a Skill Focus

1. The teacher reads several effective leads from novels or short stories.

2. Students form heterogeneous groups chosen by the teachers. One copy of a paragraph from the teacher's writing is provided for each group to read.

> This summer, I learned that teamwork and a tidal chart are very important when paddling a kayak. A friend and I decided to rent a double kayak for an afternoon outing. We set out with all the essential equipment except for a chart of the changing ocean tides, which had been left in the car. We paddled into a narrow channel. Suddenly we were traveling backwards even though we were paddling forwards. As I looked at the water churning around us I realized that we were paddling against the surging tide. *We've got to paddle harder*, I thought to myself.

3. Together each group discusses and rewrites the lead using humor, action, or dialogue so that it will capture the reader's attention.

4. The leads are shared with the class and analyzed to determine if they are effective.

5. Students edit the leads of their personal experience stories to engage their audience through humor, action, or dialogue

The Following Days

Following the first few Writers Workshop classes, the students and teachers can have a discussion about what worked well in the workshop. The students brainstorm what the class expectations are, to make the Writers Workshop a productive time for all authors.

A second area for discussion explores the kinds of questions that an author might ask during a conference with the teacher. Once a first draft of the personal experience is finished, students can request a conference with one of the teachers to get some feedback on their writing. Since conferences are designed to be short meetings between an author and a teacher, the student should come prepared with a question to ask the teacher specific to the writing.

A third discussion area is what students can do if they cannot think of a new writing topic. We often have students generate a running list of meaningful moments and experiences from their lives. They can add to and select from this list at any time.

In a conference, teachers will not have a chance to read an entire draft unless it is a short piece. These are topics that students may wish to discuss during a conference:

- lead
- use of dialogue
- development of the plot
- ending of the story
- effective imagery
- use of language
- paragraph structure; when to begin and end a paragraph

Record Keeping

Following the mini-lesson, one of the teachers records the date and topic of the composition that each of the authors is currently writing. The Status of the Class check is completed quickly so that the students can settle into their writing tasks. When a student's name is called, the topic being written and the draft number is provided for the teacher to record. As well, the teacher records if students ask for a conference during the Status of the Class check so that a conference can be scheduled during the writing period.

Many students recognize that they do their best writing in a quiet classroom with few interruptions. In one of our classes, the students took turns at the beginning of the Writers Workshop to teach the word *silence* in their first language. A Spanish-speaking boy from Mexico proudly taught the word "silencio" to his classmates and wrote the word on the board at the beginning of the writing time. The next day another student introduced the Chinese character for silence in her first language, Mandarin.

In a mini-lesson at the beginning of the year, students learn that a typical conference is about five minutes long.

During a Status of the Class check, a student response "Draft 1, holiday" notes that it is the first time a story about a holiday is written; a few days later the same student might say, "Draft 3, holiday" to indicate that two revisions have been made to the initial draft.

Status of the Class Chart

	Oct 3	Oct 10	Oct 15	Oct 17	Nov 1	Nov 14	Nov 17	Nov 21	Nov 24	Nov 28
Kamal-preet	D1 fly	D2✓© lost	©✓	comp. lost	D1 poem	D1 poem	D1 © parody	D2 parody	D2 comp.	D2 lib comp.
Gurjit	D1 lost	©✓	D1 lost	→	R.T.	D1 lost	cont'd	D1 comic	D1 cont'd	parody D2
Andrew	D1 skiing	→	D1	D2 comp.		D1 comic	D1 cont'd	D1 cont'd	→	D1
Jessica	D1 Florida	→	D1 comp.	→		D2 comp.	D2	D1 L.A.	D2 Florida comp.	D1 © L.A.
Steven	D1 lost dog	©✓		D2 comp. B-Jay		D2 comp.	D1 comic	D1 cont'd	D2 comp.	D2 comp.

D = draft
© = conference requested
New = new composition has been started; no topic yet
R.T. = resource teacher assisting student
comp. = on computer

Using the Status of the Class Chart, teachers can quickly monitor the writing being produced by each of the authors. If a student is on the first draft of a topic for a long time, one of the teachers will have a conference with the student to discuss the author's plan for ending the story. A conference is also needed for a student who keeps changing topics without completing a final draft. Students have the option to put aside a draft before it is completed; however, it is important for authors to experience the writing process by revising and editing their stories. When students are guided through the writing process, they learn how to strengthen their writing and experience the pride of completing a composition. Providing teacher support to monitor each student's progress is central to success in Writers Workshop.

The Group Share Process

A mini-lesson at the beginning of the year introduces the Group Share Process. This opportunity to share student writing may happen at any time during the workshop. All students are expected to participate by actively listening to their peers. The students who want to get feedback on their writing read a portion of their composition aloud. Students in the audience are taught to respond to the author by offering Praise, Questions, and Suggestions (PQS) pertinent to the written passage. The responses must be specific to the writing so that the feedback is useful to the author; for example, a student who offers praise by indicating that she or he liked the composition because it was funny is asked to explain the specific parts of the passage that were funny.

Using their own writing, the teachers initially model the kinds of praise, questions, and suggestions that can be made, so that the students learn how to offer feedback in a respectful and positive manner. Initially, some students may prefer to participate in the Group Share by asking one of the teachers to read their writing anonymously. Once students are familiar with this process, more of them are keen to participate by reading their writing and by offering praise, questions, and suggestions.

In some intermediate classes, over the course of a term, all students are expected to read their writing for a PQS with the entire class. As the student leads the PQS session, the classroom teacher records the feedback. When the final suggestion is given, the teacher reads back the notes so the class can edit them, ensuring the record is accurate. The notes are then given to the author to use as he/she wishes during revisions. When students internalize how to work well with PQS, they can meet in editing groups of four to follow the same process—one author reading, one recording, and the other two providing feedback.

In middle-school and secondary classrooms, Writers Workshop provides an important opportunity for teachers to build relationships with their students. Teachers get to know students through the experiences they choose to write about and the manner in which they tell their stories. Through repeated modeling and opportunities for sharing, student authors begin to take risks in sharing their personal experiences. By modeling positive feedback, a classroom community is built, based on values of trust and respect for individuality.

Mini-Lesson: Free Verse Poetry

Introducing different genres of writing during mini-lessons provides authors with new ideas for writing and expands their repertoire of ways to express their thinking. Free verse poetry is one of the mini-lessons that we teach early in the school year, since it allows students to express their ideas in an open-ended format and often appeals to writers who are challenged to write.

The following mini-lesson uses a guided walk to observe seasonal changes. Students transform their observations of nature into descriptive phrases that shape a free verse poem. Here are the steps that we follow:

1. Distribute hand-held magnifiers to pairs of students.

2. Give each student a copy of the Autumn Notes chart (page 50) to observe and record descriptive details using their senses.

3. Ask students to record as much information as they can on the chart.

4. Students walk outside, talk, and record their observations in small groups.

5. After returning to the classroom, students share a phrase or description from their observation sheets with the class.

6. Recording each idea on the overhead, the teacher builds a class list of observations.

Recording feedback allows the author to really listen to classmates without trying to remember all that is being said, and gives the author a written record of the classmates' feedback. It also places high value on the feedback and models another use of writing.

Students can record observations as descriptive phrases, words, drawings with labels, or drawings with labels and phrases explaining them.

Students may choose to borrow some of the descriptive phrases from the class list and add them to their own charts.

7. Using the class list, the teacher works with the students to determine which descriptions to include in their free verse poem.

8. Groups of students work together to make decisions about how to order the descriptive phrases for a free verse poem.

9. The finished poems are read aloud by each group.

Mini-lessons that introduce poetic conventions such as simile, metaphor, imagery, and repetition can be introduced and strengthen the skills of young poets.

10. Students share what they noticed about the order of the images in these poems.

Autumn—by Amanda

Trees are surprisingly vibrant with shades of red and yellow.
The cool tingling breeze is crisp and fresh.
A light fragrance of dew is in the morning air.
It is autumn.
Leaves gently twirling around to the brown and yellow floor.
The days are short and cool.
Birds are flying south in their orderly fashion.
Trees sway as the wind blows them swiftly.
It is autumn.
I see it.
I smell it.
I hear it.
I feel it.
It is autumn.

Fall—by Lewis

As the leaves fall gracefully to the ground like a ship slowing sinking to the misty ocean floor,
I find that I am one step closer to, but also further away from the summer that once was.
As the relaxing fall breeze flows through the street like a silent army preparing for battle,
I see the black clouds having all the power of the god called nature.
As the rain starts to slowly fall to the ground like a leaking faucet,
The streets turn to a slippery marsh of leaves.
As the murky water flows to the storm drains,
I taste the first flake of snow as it touches my tongue when this season passes once again…

Rock—by Charanpreet

Staying still like silicon
Little shiny dots like a million pieces of broken mirror
Hard like a piece of steel
Has no home
Has a life who knows
Sharp like a knife.

Autumn Notes

Sights	Sounds	Smells	Touch	Scientific Information	Other

Amanda and Lewis provide powerful autumn examples from this experience. Charanpreet also provides a powerful example, focusing on one object that he has seen on his walk. These three students represent the diversity within the classroom.

Mini-Lesson: Letting Pictures Tell the Story

When students struggle to write a narrative story, Letting Pictures Tell the Story is one of our favorite strategies to motivate writing. This strategy is designed for use with a whole class, small groups, or individual students.

1. Ask students to fold a piece of paper into six sections.

2. The teacher chooses six words that will have emotional appeal to the students, or words that have curricular connections to a unit of study: for example, *escape, hidden, determination, hope, separation, equality.*

3. Students hear the first word, and for one minute they draw all the images and connected ideas that they can in the first box.

4. This process is repeated until all six words have been illustrated.

5. Students compare their drawings with a partner, discussing the similarities and differences between their representations.

6. Students are asked to think about the connections between the words/illustrations and to choose at least four of them to include in a story.

ESL students may consult an electronic dictionary to help them decide what to draw.

Remind students that, in addition to the four words, the story should include characters, conflict, a climax, and a resolution.

It just isn't fair. Nothing's fair, Martin thought sullenly, sitting in detention. *Just because I wrote an essay he didn't like. I get detention?* He looked around the room in vain for <u>hope</u> of <u>escape</u>. It was a warm and sunny day, a perfect day to be outside. A teacher, Mr. McKeal, walked in, interrupting his thoughts.

"Hello, Martin. Now what did you do today?"

"Nothing," Martin said defensively. "We were all supposed to write an essay about what we think is important in life, and then read it out loud to the whole class. I wrote about <u>equality</u>, and after I read it out loud, Mr. Green started making stupid suggestions. I got angry and said something, so he sent me here."

Mr. McKeal raised his eyebrows. "Oh, really? Mr. Green said you wrote something inappropriate, and he was just trying to help you. Then you started yelling at him."

Martin started to protest, but was cut off by a gesture by Mr. McKeal's hand. "The way I see it, you were being inexcusably rude to your teacher. Although Mr. Green may not have been able to share your point of view, you should have held back your anger. As your punishment, you will write a hundred word essay to apologize to your teacher. Next time, I'd suggest you write something your teacher agrees on. Okay?" When Martin nodded, Mr. McKeal dismissed him.

Frustrated, Martin ran out of the school. *Nobody understands. They're all too narrow-minded.* Taking a deep breath of the fresh autumn air, he made up his mind. Blazing with <u>determination</u>, he made a silent vow. *One day,* he thought, *one day I'll write an essay about what I believe in that they will never, ever forget.*

Mini-Lesson: Power Paragraphs for Information Writing

Early in the school year we teach students how to communicate ideas and information using the Power Paragraph format. The Power Paragraph graphic organizer (page 54) is designed to help students choose a main idea, include relevant facts and supporting details, and write them in a logical order. We start with one paragraph and, as the students' proficiency grows, we add more paragraphs to expand on the topic. Before long, the students are able to write short essays to communicate their ideas about a topic.

1. Students receive a copy of the Power Paragraph graphic organizer (page 54).

2. A compelling article is chosen for the students to read on their own or with support, as needed.

3. Working in pairs, students discuss what struck them about the article; e.g., something that surprised them, something they learned, something they would like to know more about.

4. Students then work as a class to choose one fact or big idea in the article. This is recorded in point form on the graphic organizer on the overhead.

5. Students, as a class, reread the article to find two details that support or tell more about the fact or big idea. These are added in point form to the graphic organizer.

6. Students continue working in pairs to identify the second fact and supporting details, and record this information on the graphic organizer.

7. Students continue the process to identify and record a third fact with supporting details.

8. Students move into small groups to review the three facts and supporting details. They work together to construct a topic sentence for the paragraph that introduces the topic in an interesting way.

9. Each group shares their topic sentence so the class can determine which of the sentences is the most effective.

10. Working with a partner, students weave the ideas in the first fact and the supporting details into one or two complete sentences, using connecting words such as *and, but, so, because,* and *therefore.*

11. This process is repeated until the facts and details have all been rewritten into complete sentences.

12. The topic sentence is reread and edited, if needed, to fit the rest of the sentences in the paragraph.

13. Decisions are made by each student as to the order in which the sentences are best presented

14. Starting with the topic sentence, the entire paragraph is written. It can now be edited or proofread, as required.

Power Paragraph

Topic Sentence

Fact 1

Fact 2

Fact 3

Detail

Detail

Detail

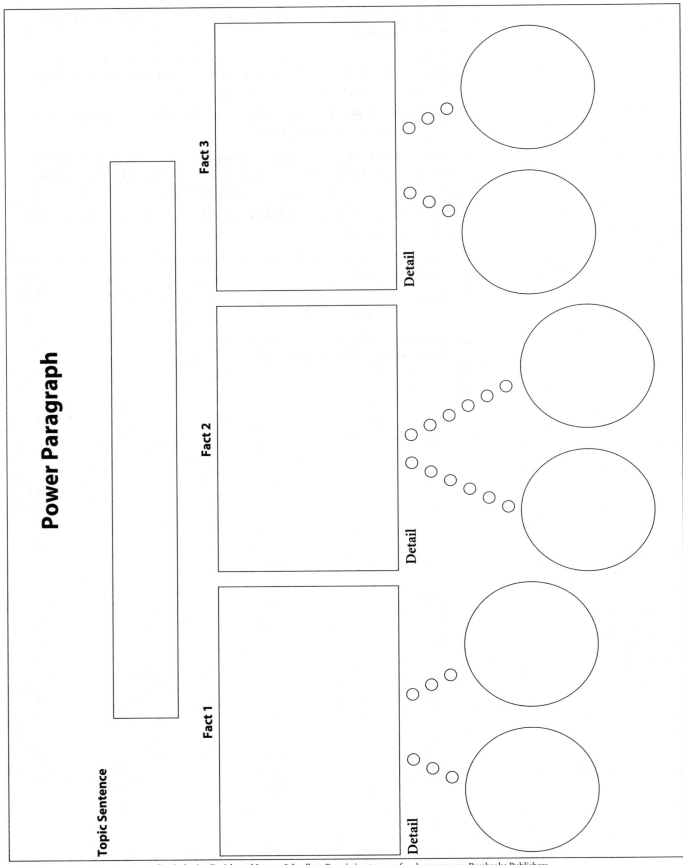

5 Introducing Narrative Writing

In this chapter, Leyton, as resource teacher, collaborated with four Grades 6/7 classroom teachers who shared these beliefs during the first term of the school year, to engage middle-years writers in improving their writing while becoming "self-" and "other-wise."

We herald the importance of teacher collaboration. We are passionate in our belief that students learn better in classroom communities where they feel they belong. We believe all students can be and should be included in ways that improve the learning of all students. We believe that writing is the foundation from which our classrooms grow as learning communities.

The initial questions of our Grades 6/7 teachers had propelled them into an inquiry project that shaped their instruction for the term.

> Chris Loat: "How can I streamline my writing program to help all of my students feel more successful? I have many strategies for writing but I don't think all of my students are reaching their potential."

> Rick Hikida: "How can I help my students generalize the skills and knowledge they learn from one piece to the next? I have tried to introduce the Performance Standards to the students, but it doesn't seem to make a difference."

> Andrea Western/Cesca Juhasz (job-share partners): "How can we achieve a balance between choice and demand topics? Our students write well when given a topic, but struggle with significantly less powerful writing when choosing a topic of their own."

We were already committed to the writing process. Planning and teaching together, however, gave us an opportunity to refine our skills and better address the needs of our diverse groups of students.

We met on the last day of school in June and sketched out our plan for the following fall. We knew that our incoming group of students had trouble getting along, so we decided that weaving in aspects of social responsibility and perspective taking would be crucial for a successful school year. The school had already been working on developing a school-wide effective behavior support plan, and so we planned to embody the acronym STAR (Safety, Teamwork, Accountability, Respect), adopted by the school, in our lessons and interactions with the students. We decided to begin the fall with personal/impromptu writing that would allow us to get to know the students—each individual's point of view and interests—while focusing on meaning and ideas in their writing. We chose the topic of "Belonging" for the first term.

Our available resource time was minimal—one 80-minute block per class per week. This time was used for co-teaching. Often, the resource teacher would model an anchor lesson in one of the classes. Following the anchor lesson, the classroom teachers shared what had happened, then worked with the same idea twice more before the next anchor lesson a week later. Each anchor lesson included

- time for a mini-lesson

As a starting point, we reread chapter 3 on "Belonging" from Brownlie and King's *Learning In Safe Schools* (2000) and adapted some of their activities for our classes.

- time for students to begin writing
- time for students sharing excerpts from their work in progress

The writing blocks between anchor lessons were usually 40 minutes each, with a quick review of the anchor lesson and time to write and share.

Week One: Pre-writing

Anchor Lesson: Getting to Feelings and Emotions Through Pre-writing

We felt the brainstorm was important in order to show several things:
- one possible way to organize thinking;
- that one can belong in different ways;
- that in brainstorming one can add details and explanations to original ideas.

1. As resource teacher, I modeled a brainstorm/braindrain on "What belonging means to me," giving examples from my life of places, activities, and people that made me feel like I belonged. I tried to cover a variety of areas that students could relate to—sports, music, religion, family, school, leisure activities. Modeling the inclusion of the fullest range of places and people helped students tap into the same things.

2. Students generated their own personal brainstorm/ braindrain on "Belonging."

3. I used a different color to write how each of my points made me feel, then students did the same on their brainstorms.

Gel pens were all the rage, so switching colors was a thrill for the class!

4. I circled the three ideas that I thought were my best, most powerful ideas, and had the students circle their three best ideas.

5. Students took out a third color. They shared and discussed their top three examples with the others in their table group of four. With the new color, students added to their brainstorm ideas that came up in the group.

6. Students were given the journal topic "What does belonging mean to me?" I modeled writing on the overhead and asked the students to write their own pieces.

7. I quickly finished my piece and then, with the other teacher, circulated around the room to nudge students who needed assistance in getting started, often referring to the example on the overhead.

We learned a great deal from observing students' writing. For example, after the first week Cesca and Andrea noted the following:

Class writing strengths:

— they enjoy writing
— excited to talk about social issues and real-life situations
— have a lot of ideas/things to write about
— no one was sitting staring at their paper saying, "I have nothing to write about…"

Areas to work on:

— they use very simple vocabulary (e.g., *nice, mean, sad*)
— getting more depth/feeling in their writing (many would express ideas orally but did not convey that same sense in their writing)

Over the course of the next week, entries were written on friendship: "What does being a good friend look like? Sound like? Feel like?"

After the first week, we decided to develop criteria with students to help address their writing needs and our inquiry questions. We would spend the next six to eight weeks gently developing criteria with the students.

Week Two: Writing Criteria

Anchor Lesson: Analyzing Peer Writing for Strengths

Once students internalize and articulate what makes powerful personal/impromptu/journal writing, they should apply these criteria, writing fluently and confidently without stopping too often to attend to criteria.

1. With the What Makes a Powerful Journal Entry? graphic organizer (page 59) in front of them, we looked at three student samples pre-selected by the classroom teacher, analyzing them to determine what makes a powerful journal entry. These samples were from a range of ability levels, each showing something powerful.

2. As we looked at the samples, we asked students to find some that made each journal entry powerful. Students then individually put the aspects that they thought were most important in the "My Ideas" section of the graphic organizer. We asked students to circle or otherwise mark their criteria to rate the first three in order of importance.

3. In table groups of four, students shared their ideas and recorded them in the "Group Ideas" section of the graphic organizer. Groups then came to consensus on their top three criteria, and shared these with the class. These were recorded in the "Class Ideas" section.

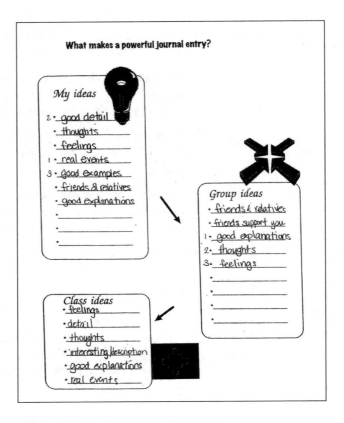

4. After discussing the criteria, students brainstormed and wrote journal entries on "What can belonging look like and feel like in our classroom?"

Class Lessons

Using the criteria that the students had generated, each teacher created their own follow-up lessons, designed to address the needs of their particular class.

Criteria for Powerful Writing: Andrea/Cesca's class

Cesca and Andrea's class looked at more student samples and came up with two or three powerful things about each person's writing sample. They wrote in their journals after discussing the criteria again. Cesca had three students display the criteria on a poster.

- put your own feelings into it
- have details
- use your imagination
- use a variety of words
- interest the reader
- has a beginning, middle, and an ending
- own original ideas
- exciting
- strong words and ideas
- consistently written (strong/powerful all the way through)

What Makes a Powerful Journal Entry?

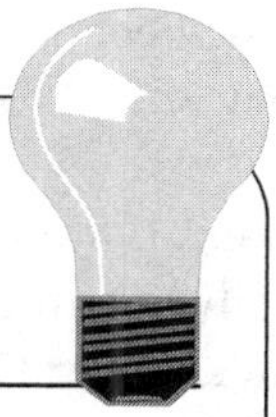

My ideas

* _____
* _____
* _____
* _____
* _____
* _____
* _____
* _____
* _____

Group ideas

* _____
* _____
* _____
* _____
* _____
* _____
* _____
* _____
* _____

Class ideas

* _____
* _____
* _____
* _____
* _____
* _____

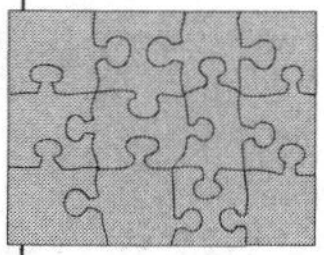

Keeping a Focus: Rick's class

Rick decided to do an anchor lesson to help students stay focused within their paragraphs. He showed a picture of a professional hockey player scoring a goal. He asked students to infer and brainstorm what they knew about the picture and wrote their ideas on the board. Then he modeled writing a paragraph using their ideas from the board while keeping the image of the hockey game on the overhead screen. As a class they added to his paragraph and read it aloud several times.

Once he completed the paragraph of the hockey game, he slid a picture of Long Neck Fred, one of Shel Silverstein's cartoon characters, into the hockey scene. The students had a chuckle over this. Rick asked the question, "Does Long Neck Fred belong here?" After much discussion, Rick explained that this is what some of the students' paragraphs looked like. There were sentences or ideas that did not belong in the context of the specific paragraph, and should have been included in another paragraph or a new journal topic all together. It was a visual way of showing them what a proper paragraph should look like.

Transferring Skills: Chris's class

Chris found that students had some very insightful thoughts and ideas that they were trying to express; however, many did not seem to be able to express their thoughts in very descriptive or meaningful ways. The word "good" seemed to come up far too often. They finished their "Belonging in the Classroom" journal entry and worked on another journal response about friendship. Chris and his class discussed the criteria and, during each writing session, he asked students to point out the criteria they felt were important. Chris emphasized that these were the criteria that they should be thinking about when doing their written responses. However, after perusing a few of the responses, he found that some of the students did not seem to know exactly what some of the criteria—such as use of detail and providing good explanations—referred to.

Chris also noticed that during other written assignments, such as a major Social Studies activity, the students did not seem to realize that the writing process should be applied to their responses: the students immediately began a good copy response without any planning or drafting. Chris stopped the whole class and told them that, for this fairly major assignment, he expected some sort of pre-writing with later revision. Their blank stares of bewilderment at this were telling, as we realized the lack of carry-over in student writing processes from subject to subject.

After two weeks, we were pleased to note that some of the students seemed to be writing in organized paragraphs or sections without a receiving a mini-lesson on the topic. Some had even started organizing their work into sections with subtitles. By simply surfacing and emphasizing the criteria, students had begun to move away from writing one long, drawn-out paragraph.

Week Three: Group Work

Anchor Lesson: Sorting and Categorizing Criteria

1. Each group of four students was given an envelope containing the powerful-journal criteria brainstormed the week before. Each idea was typed on its

---

Students need to build criteria, then practise writing and revising with the criteria in mind, to become more powerful writers.

We came up with easy to remember names for the criteria:

Final Touch: good sentences, organized, easy to read, neatness

Thinking It Through: feelings, pictures/drawings, thoughts, real events

Sounds Great: exciting, good explanations, interesting/description, detail, good use of words

own strip of paper. Students had to deduce which ideas went together and come up with a reason or title for each group. We had a copy of the strips on overhead acetate.

2. As a class we analyzed each group's proposal, focusing on which criteria went together, and listed the titles on the overhead. We chose the titles that worked best for the class and left them on the overhead. The groups went back and regrouped the criteria using the same process. Each group chose the criteria that they were most certain about and shared their reasoning with the class. Following the students' suggestions, I arranged and rearranged the criteria under the various headings.

3. We asked the students to spend five minutes discussing how effectively they worked as a group.

4. Students then wrote a journal entry responding to the prompt, "How do good groups work?"

Class Lessons

The teachers used the prompts "What makes you a good friend?" and "How can a group make good decisions?" for the week's journal writes. They continued to ask students to choose and focus on two or three criteria for each write, and gave mini-lessons on specific skills, as needed.

Week Four: Using the Criteria

To prepare for this lesson the teachers asked their students to identify a piece of their own writing that they believed met one of the criteria categories particularly well. By this time students had at least six entries to choose from, and many of them spent more than an hour choosing which piece to use. Those students who struggled with this process sat in partners or small groups with a teacher reading their pieces aloud and helping them discuss which criteria they believed had been met. This prepared them for the next anchor lesson when they would continue to use the criteria with their writing.

Anchor Lesson: The Art of Noticing

1. I read one of my draft pieces of writing from the overhead. I referred to the posted criteria and read my piece again, looking for an example of one of the criteria.

2. Working in partners, students looked for other examples of the criteria in my piece. We debriefed, and the pairs of students came up to underline a relevant section and label it with the criteria.

3. Students brought out the piece that they had selected. Using a colored pen, they underlined phrases or sentences that they believed demonstrated a criteria, and wrote this criteria beside it.

4. Each student shared a quote, and the class guessed which criteria it was an example of.

5. Students described what they had noticed about their thinking and chose one of the criteria to focus on in their next piece.

Journal

Title: What does it look & feel like to belong in a group?   **Teacher Comments**

To belong to a group feels great. Everyone knows your name, welcomes you and hangs out with you. In my group of friends I feel that everyone understands me and cares. When I'm in a class like, for example, Judo class, everyone recognizes me and feels challenged and excited to learn new skills together. In my family, I feel loved and cared for. I also look a lot like my dad. When I joined a get-together once, there was no one I knew in the crowd. I was going to leave until I saw my friend and her sister. I stayed and we had lots of fun together. In the school band I feel like I belong because everyone there knows how to play an instrument, and we're all being

Teacher comments (right column): feelings / Good Thoughts Explanations / Real Events Details

Some students benefited more by returning to finish a piece rather than starting a new one. Our requirement was that each student had at least one piece a week to work with for the anchor lesson.

Class Lessons

During the next week teachers had students look for examples of criteria in their writing and required students to set a goal related to the criteria before each write.

Week Five: Revising

Anchor Lesson: Making Revisions in Your Writing

> Reivisng is using criteria to help your reader get your written message.

We had been focusing on building student confidence, raising awareness of strength in each and every student's writing, and the development of criteria in "kid friendly" language. To prepare for working on the concept of revision, I took the criteria and titles and made a graphic organizer for students. Now that we had developed their critical eye for linking criteria to example, we wanted to move students into using this criteria to revise their work. We defined revising as using criteria to determine how I, as a writer, might better get my message across.

1. I explained that, as a writer, I am constantly revising aspects of my writing. I choose a piece or an aspect of my writing that I am excited about and I think about what I know about powerful writing—my criteria—to see if I can make it better.

2. I modeled the process of choosing one really good sentence from my piece. I explained that I was looking for phrases that are or could be descriptive/ powerful phrases.

3. I read the first chunk of my piece several times before choosing a sentence to focus on.

   > Deep, honest, complex… My friend Kara and her husband have a lot on their plate with a baby coming and the restaurant's grand opening on the 22nd.

   I wrote this sentence in the "Good Start" section of my graphic organizer.

4. Students were partnered A/B. Partners were asked what they thought could be done to make my sentence more descriptive. I thought aloud and shared what I thought I could do. Then, I revised my sentence using their advice and wrote it in the "Even Better" section.

5. Each student found a quote from his/her piece and shared with the partner, telling what they chose and how they would change it.

6. We repeated this oral rehearsal process. Then students chose this or another sentence to write in the organizer and revise.

7. We finished the class by having students share the first and revised versions of their sentences.

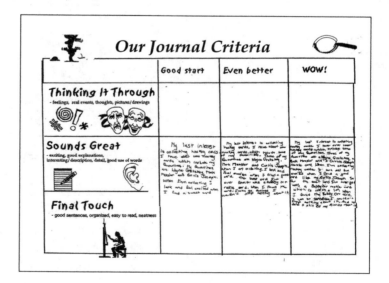

Class Lessons

Up to and including this point, no marks had been given. We were in assessment-*for*-learning mode. Students did not submit pieces for evaluation (marks) until the end of the term.

Students continued to write and revise aspects of their piece over the next week. Teachers had to conference with students before they could revise their sentence(s) a second time and take them to the WOW stage. Students then conferenced on each other's work to describe what kinds of revisions had been done. Finally, they went back to the section of the piece that their sentence was from and revised the section in reference to a category of the criteria. They handed the revisions in to the teacher. These pieces let us know what we needed to focus on next with our mini-lessons; they let us give students specific feedback on how they were doing according to our specific goals, and how they could get better.

Week Six: Choosing Topics

Anchor Lesson: Graffiti and Conversation

We wanted to stimulate more discussion regarding content, and to reinforce that writers need passion for their topic and voice in their writing. We also wanted to begin to have more student choice of writing prompts.

1. We reviewed the criteria as a class. We gave students a choice of two criteria categories to target: meaning- and style-based categories.

2. The class was divided into six groups. Each group was given a "graffiti palette" (a large piece of butcher paper) with a different "Belonging" prompt in the centre. Students had between five and ten minutes to brainstorm their reactions, examples, and details to the prompt on the graffiti palette before rotating to the next topic. Students returned to their original palette after three rotations.

3. Students examined the results, taking turns reading quotes from the graffiti.

4. Each student then chose one of the prompts to write on independently.

Prompts included
- *Imagine what a school would be like if all children felt they belonged.*
- *Tell about a time when you were judged.*
- *Tell about a time you didn't belong.*
- *Describe what cooperation means.*
- *Think about how this school includes everyone.*
- *Imagine what being new in this class would be like.*

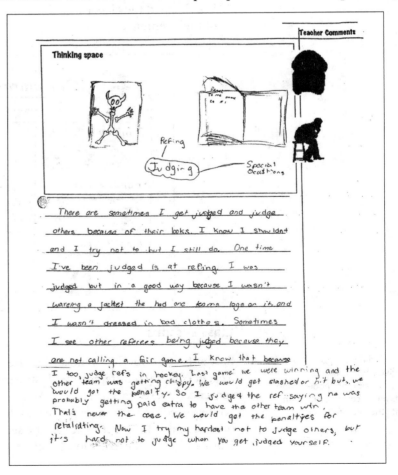

Journal Organizer

Prompt:

Name:

Date:

Teacher Comments

Thinking space

Div. 1 Peace Journal Topics	**Possible topics cont'd**
I get angry when....	Do you think that fighting with each other helps us realize why peace is important?
I feel peaceful when.....	Be helpful, don't be greedy.
If Hitler never existed, how would the world be different?	Will racism lead to peace?
If peace was a law, would you obey it?	How do you feel about Sept. 11th?
Will the world ever have total peace?	How do you feel about enemies?
Do you think that wars between countries end in peace?	How do you feel about bombing Afghanistan?
Do you think that the war between terrorism and the US will end in peace?	How do you feel about friendship?
Do you think the world will be without wars?	Do you want to help the world?
Will terrorism ever end?	Do you want to help starving people? people in need? the homeless? sick people? orphans? the Red Cross victims?
Can war ever result in peace?	Why is the world like this?
Do you think that everyone in schools wearing uniforms would stop bullying?	Why is Bin Laden like this?
Do you think that you have a reason to revolutionize the world in peace?	Why is America like this?
If you were able to change anything in the world, what would it be?	Why are there evil people?
If money did not exist would the world have peace?	Why is there war?
Make peace, not war.	Do you care about people with disabilities?
Make friends, not war.	What do you want to do about the world?
What is peace?	What do you want to do about wars?
What is war?	What do you want to do about Bin Laden?
What is love?	If I could change something, it would be... (how people think about each other, sin, etc.)
What are friends?	What is your vision of peace?
What is a perfect world?	What would a non-racist world look like?
What is freedom?	If the terrorist attack never happened, do you think there would be more peace in the world?
Do people think better of themselves or of each other?	If there were less killing, would there be more peace in the world?
Do weapons help create peace?	Do you think peace should be a right? Why or why not?
How can we heal the world?	What do you think is achieved from war?
Will war become helpful?	Pray for peace, not war.
Will terrorists rule the world?	Should America make peace or war with Afghanistan?
War will not settle anything.	Why or why not?
Do you care more about war than peace?	Do you think spending millions making weapons is going to make peace?
Do you think childrens' lives will be affected by war?	
If you could make world peace, would you?	
Do you think terrorists care?	
I used to think that peace was.........but now I know that peace is.......	
What do you think the world would be like without peace?	
Do you think countries resolve their differences in war and fighting? Why or why not?	
What positive things have been achieved since Sept. 11, 2001?	
What do you think 'peace' means? Why?	
Do you think the Americans are overreacting?	
Do you think the Americans are trying to promote peace or war?	
Should America look to others for guidance?	
If you were in the Americans' shoes, what would you do?	
Should other countries attack Afghanistan?	
Should Canada join in the fight with the US?	
If you had a chance to kill Bin Laden, would you?	
Should we use germ warfare?	

5. We used the Journal Organizer on page 65, with a thinking space for drawing, listing, mindmapping.

Class Lessons

Our Grades 6/7 team brainstormed related themes for the rest of the term and chose "Peace/Piece" as a fun and relevant twin focus. As students were now familiar with the routines of journaling and felt an ownership of the criteria, we asked each class to brainstorm a list of powerful journal topics related to the concept of peace. On page 66 is the impressive list from one of the classes. Notice how almost all of the ideas are not only powerful but are posed as prompts.

Week Seven: Using Form Effectively

Anchor Lesson: Cracking Open Your Topic and Getting Beyond Listing

After reading through the first peace journals we decided that a very targeted mini-lesson was in order. Students were doing a good job including details and emotions, but the pieces almost read like lists. Students were not fully expanding their ideas. We also noticed that most pieces did not have a satisfying ending. We realized that we had supported the students in writing multi-paragraph pieces, but needed to have a targeted lesson on ways to use form effectively.

1. We chose two magazine articles that had effective leads and endings and told the story of one key moment. We read these and discussed their form.

2. We looked at the list of peace topics generated. In partners, students discussed how to choose a topic that would yield the best personal writing.

3. I modeled an initial web about my chosen topic, getting down several possible ideas. The students chose a topic from the peace prompt list and did the same.

4. I returned to my web and thought aloud about which of my ideas I had really strong examples for. I wrote down the powerful example, explaining the connection between the prompt and my idea. I explained that one strong personal example is the skeleton for the entire piece. I generated several possible leads, and started my piece on the overhead.

5. Students wrote their entries.

Students easily chose a topic and began to brainstorm ideas. We were impressed with the quality of questions and the variety of ideas around the theme of peace. When it came time to write, they all were able to get ideas down on paper. Some of them were really focusing on powerful, catchy beginnings, detailed middles and endings that tied up their writing.

> Using a key moment to build on with description and detail will yield a much stronger piece than a list.

Class Lessons

The mini-lesson really seemed to sink in for many of the students. However, given some of the topics, it was difficult for them to focus only on one example, rather than to give a list. Some of the students didn't have enough background knowledge or information to write in detail about one example. This became something to focus on for the next week: choosing a topic that students had a strong opinion about or examples to use in their writing.

The teachers re-emphasized that we wanted to stretch out a moment and work on adding details in our personal writing. They also modeled effective endings and had students examine and rework their leads and endings. The classes decided that effective endings included opinions, questions, and observations.

Whenever Writer Workshop time was scheduled, the students had a focus. They were getting better at choosing a topic, and were coming up with personal stories or illustrative examples. Teachers and students concluded that writing more than one extended example helped create a powerful, longer entry.

Week Eight: Establishing Criteria for Evaluation

As we moved toward the end of the term, we could see how our identifying patterns in our students' writing led to focused mini-lessons which in turn resulted in immediate improvement in the students' writing. Targeted teaching was making a difference!

Anchor Lesson: Getting Ready for Evaluation

Our provincial Performance Standards for Writing were used by the teachers as a second set of criteria.

1. Each teacher and class revisited the criteria and the original categories and refined them. With the students, we looked at the two sets of criteria—our revised criteria and the provincial performance standards—to see where there was overlap.

2. We combined the criteria into one master set of criteria as a class. We asked the students what they thought we should add to the criteria based on our recent mini-lessons. In the end we had a category and descriptors that matched each of the four aspects of writing on the performance standards, each built by looking at pieces by us and other authors.

The students had absolute ownership over their own set of criteria. We believe that the power of generating criteria over time is one of the key reasons that students steadily improved. They had determined the descriptors, constantly worked towards the criteria, and now had refined them.

3. To parallel the performance standards, we added a fourth column into our Good Start, Getting There, WOW rubric, and called it "I'm There." We clarified what a strong piece would include, and put these descriptors in the "I'm There" column.

Our Journal Criteria

	Good start	Even better	I'm There	WOW!
Thinking It Through feelings, thoughts & opinions real events explanations & details personal experiences			• fully explains why you have these opinions, thoughts or feelings • feelings and thoughts fully support the topic • reader clearly understands the thoughts/opinions of the writer • deeper level of thinking that shows insight and individuality	
Sounds Great description good use of words clear explanations varied length of sentences			• uses clear and varied vocabulary • variety of sentence length and structure • language helps the reader understand the ideas and thoughts of the writer	
Get Up & Organized well organized ideas interesting beginning well developed middle powerful ending one main idea in each paragraph			• ideas flow from one to another in a logical sequence • interesting beginning • well developed middle • powerful ending • related ideas are grouped together	
Final Touch sentences - mechanically correct COPS			• most sentences are grammatically correct • few errors in capitalization, punctuation and spelling • errors do not interfere with the meaning of the journal	

Mr Loat's grade 6/7 class

4. Once the categories and descriptors were revised, the students looked at some of their own work to find samples that fit the specific criteria.

Evaluation

About five weeks into the process, we had explained to students that they would be selecting three pieces to take to an almost published form. Evaluation of these, combined with that of a "demand write," would constitute their writing mark for the term. We reviewed the rubric with the class. Then students were given a copy of the rubric to refer to while they were finalizing their writing.

We evaluated the following:

1. A journal entry that they worked through the three stages—taking their writing from a "Good Start" to "Even Better," and finally to "I'm There."

2. An in-class write. If students needed additional time to finish, we blocked off extra time in class.

Most students chose pieces that they had already revised parts of during our various mini-lessons.

Thinking Back, Looking Ahead

We were thrilled by the progress of our three classes of students. While developing an understanding of what is important in personal/impromptu writing, they also learned how to analyze their own writing with specific criteria in mind. The students demonstrated a good understanding of the rubric that we came up with collaboratively.

Journal writing continued throughout the year; however, in term two we shifted our focus to story writing and found the process of generating criteria and building a rubric to take far less time. Students were amazed to find that many of the criteria were the same and that all of the criteria categories were similar. As we moved through the term, targeting and modeling specific aspects of writing in our mini-lessons, we found that students were more successful in revising their writing. This was especially true for some of our struggling writers. Our explicitness about what worked in writing, building from what was missing in their writing, was most beneficial to them.

One of our inquiry questions seemed to answer itself, as students themselves began to point out the importance of the skills and the transferability of the criteria from piece to piece and genre to genre. We had learned to take the time to work together. In addition to partners, our classes could also work in trios and quartets. Through our topic of "Belonging" we were able to bring to the surface what each of us believed belonging to be and how this applied in the classroom, on the playground, and in our personal lives. We, as teachers, discovered that we were more comfortable slowing down and focusing on developing key skills. Finally, we all had begun to ask one another for the reasons behind our examples, our actions, and our statements. We were all learning to look for our expanded stories, instead of just creating lists.

6 The Class Novel

What Was

Choosing one novel for all students is based on the belief that, if everyone is doing the same thing, all are included.

In our intermediate and middle-years classes, the class novel has too often become the backbone of the English/Language Arts program. Teaching a novel usually means analysis and close examination of literary elements, such as the plot line, the author's intent, and literary techniques. A whole class novel is manageable. The same assignments are used for everyone. Everyone is working at the same time, in the same place, at the same pace. It is traditional. It takes up time.

We believe that the time has passed when one size fits all. One of the challenges of today's diverse classes is that, when a teacher chooses one novel for the entire class, rarely can all the students actually read the novel. So the teacher, in an attempt to include everyone in discussions about the novel, reads it to them, chapter by chapter. Two things then happen:

- a great deal of time is devoured
- most students engage in almost no actual reading

Neither of these results promote personal growth in reading. Nor do they create conditions for developing an enthusiasm for and a love of reading. The more-able readers are bored, the less-able readers are dormant.

What Can Be

Novel study can be a worthy activity if it is
- brief
- well-introduced
- adapted to the class needs
- encouraging and supporting students' independent reading

We do believe that teaching a novel to the entire class is a worthy activity. However, we have come to rely on a set of beliefs for this teaching:

- The novel study should take three to four weeks at a maximum, as there simply isn't enough reading time for students otherwise.
- The novel needs to be introduced in a way that sets up all students to want to read it and be more able to read it.
- Not every chapter needs to be processed in the same depth; i.e., assigned a strategy, discussed, worked over.
- Not every literary technique or comprehension strategy needs to be covered in every novel. Teachers choose a theme, a technique, or a focus, and address this in one novel, knowing that they can address other curriculum goals using another novel.
- Students need to read independently as much as they can.
- Comprehension questions, chapter by chapter, take up valuable time and teach nothing.

- The purpose of a novel study is to become engrossed in a good read, not to do "stuff" like comprehension questions and book reports.
- A whole-class novel is an appropriate time to introduce, teach, model, and practise a reading/thinking strategy that students can later use in their independent reading.

Connecting: Building Background

Several strategies build background knowledge and increase a student's interest and motivation to read. Teachers may choose to use one or more of these strategies, depending on the needs of their students. They are usually the students' first introduction to the novel, and precede naming the text or any preamble about it.

Gallery Walk

1. Collect a series of images or artifacts that represent the setting of the novel, or things that are particularly important to the characters in the novel. Place them around the room, arranged so that students in groups of three can meet to examine them: i.e., for a class of 30 students, you would display ten items.

2. In groups of three, students discuss what they are seeing and what it might tell them about the novel. Students spend about three minutes at each item. Students do not need to see all artifacts—visiting four is plenty.

3. Upon returning to their seats, students write for ten minutes, explaining what they think they now know about the novel.

4. Student writing is shared with all the images or artifacts are displayed, so students can predict which images or artifacts each author actually examined.

Historical Picture Book

1. Choose a picture book that builds background knowledge about a novel whose setting is not well-known to the students in the class. This can be either historical (When) or geographic (Where).

2. As you read the picture book, show the pictures and discuss the language and the images with the students.

3. Read the picture book again, focusing the students on two aspects and making two-column notes:

   Historical or Geographic Fact   My Connections

4. Students can work in pairs to embellish their notes, highlighting and noting three to five aspects of either history (When) or geography (Where).

5. Hear at least one response from each pair, building a class web focusing on either the When or the Where information.

Choice Beginnings

1. Choose 15 to 20 image-producing words from the novel. Tell students that you are going to read a series of image-producing words from the upcoming novel, and invite them to respond to these words by asking questions, making predictions, or sketching.

2. Invite students to predict which response format they are most likely to use and to tell this to a partner.

3. Read the words to the students several times, inviting them to listen and respond as they are ready. Plan on reading the words as often as five or six times, encouraging the students to NOT copy down the words, but listen and respond to them.

4. Check to see how many students expected to respond in one way, then responded in another. Hear some of the questions and predictions, and see some of the images.

Processing: Building Meaning

These strategies bear repeating, so students gain skill in using the thinking behind the strategy in their independent reading. However, it is inappropriate to work with a strategy with each and every chapter. That means too much teaching and too little time supporting students in working toward independence as thoughtful readers.

Once some background and motivation has been built, some classes are able to begin independently reading the novel. However, other classes demand more teacher support with the language, structure, style, or background knowledge needed to fully understand the novel. If this is the case, the first chapter might be read aloud by the teacher, while the students engage in one of the strategies outlined here. These strategies can also be relevant later in the novel, with the teacher reading aloud a chapter or a segment of a chapter that requires additional teaching.

For Quadrants of a Thought as part of a strategic sequence, see page 17 in chapter 1.

Quadrants of a Thought

1. Students fold a piece of paper in four and label the quadrants **Image**, **Language**, **Physical Senses**, and **Emotions**.

2. As the teacher reads, students are invited to record, in two of the four boxes, what is going on in their minds about the text. Students will sketch in the **Image** quadrant; record significant words, phrases, or quotes in the **Language** quadrant; record sounds, smells, the sense of touch or movement, and tastes in the **Physical Senses** quadrant; and note the emotional reactions of either themselves or the characters in the **Emotions** quadrant.

Filling in two quadrants is enough to begin with, and will grow with practice to include all four quadrants.

3. Read one or two pages of the text, then stop and hear what students have been recording.

4. Make a quadrant on the overhead and record the student responses. Students are not required to copy down what is on the overhead, but may use any of the ideas there, as they wish.

5. Continue the process, stopping again, adding to the class recording. Ask the students to be noticing what is changing in their thinking and their recording as you continue.

Recording the class responses develops a whole-class appreciation of what others are thinking and helps develop a greater understanding of personal connections and interpretations.

6. Stop and debrief a third time, if appropriate, then read uninterrupted to the end; or assign the students to finish the chapter reading independently.

Listen/Sketch/Draft

1. Students fold a page into four or six boxes. They will use two boxes for each chunk of text, so you'll have to decide how many chunks you will be processing.

2. Read the first part of the chapter and invite students to sketch what is happening as you read.

3. Stop reading, give a few moments for the sketching to finish, then invite students to share their sketches and their thinking with a partner.

4. Hear samples of the partners' conversations by asking the question, "What surprised you about your partner's thinking?" or "What did your partner do differently from you?" or "What do you know now that you didn't before your conversation?"

5. Students quickly record, in writing, what is important to remember in the first chunk of text.

6. Continue this process for one or two more chunks, then have students complete the reading of the first chapter independently.

Clustering from Text

Students looking for more ideas may ask you to reread the text.

1. Read the first few pages of the text to the students. As you read, invite students to quickly cluster their thinking about the text, important words from the text, and their connections to the text.

2. Ask students to circle two powerful words in their cluster.

3. Use these powerful words to make a class cluster on the board. Invite each student to be prepared to contribute.

4. As students contribute their ideas, remind them that you can record, but you cannot read their minds, so they need to tell you where to place each idea; i.e., students are categorizing as they build the class cluster.

Students are encouraged to contribute an idea, to categorize or connect this idea to others, and to explain why they placed the idea where they did. We call this "because" thinking.

5. When all have contributed and the board is full, take out colored chalk or colored overhead pens. Each student now has a chance to rearrange the cluster by connecting words that were not previously connected and explaining their relationship. This part of the strategy really deepens understanding.

6. Once the cluster is "messed up" and most of the words have been reconnected, students write for ten minutes in response to what has been read. Expect the writing to demonstrate a thoughtful, connected, powerful understanding.

During Reading

Partner Reading

The intent is to move through the novel more quickly than in the past, and also to increase the amount of time students actually engage in reading.

If students still cannot independently read the text, we place the students in reading partners for the duration of a class novel. When assigning a chapter or two to read, the partners work together during class time. The rule is that they need to arrange a way of reading that ensures that each partner reads at least some of every second page—even if it is only a line! We set up the partnerships, considering social issues (who can work with whom) and reading skill (in each partnership, one person needs to be able to read longer passages). As the students are reading, we move among the partners, listening in and supporting as needed.

Sticky Notes

Sometimes the students just mark the spot with their sticky notes; more often they write or draw on them.

We encourage students to read with sticky notes in hand, distributing them to the partner groups. Their task, as they read, is to use the sticky notes to mark places in the text where

- there is exquisite language
- a strong emotion is evoked
- a clear image is created
- they are confused and need to ask a question
- they say, "Oh, wow!"
- they find a phrase they want to use

Students take the sticky note from the novel and place it on their desk as they speak. Then, at a glance, we all can tell who has not yet had a chance to speak and who has.

This tiny strategy causes a great deal of literate conversation to occur. When the partners are finished reading, we hold a class conversation based on what is written and drawn on the sticky notes. Many more students participate in this whole-class conversation, because they have already rehearsed with their partners. The conversation is less likely to be controlled by a verbal few. We begin our conversations each time with a different focus, sometimes beginning with the "Oh, Wow!" statements, sometimes with the images, sometimes with the questions. Again, this changes who begins first in the conversation.

Response Journals

After the class conversation, we move to writing in response journals. All students are more able to participate in writing a thoughtful response, because they have been supported before the writing, rather than getting feedback after the writing.

We do not ask comprehension questions as we are progressing through the novel. These are not supportive of developing more thoughtful readers or of increasing reading skill. They are the stuff that kills reading by over-monitoring. They are not real questions, as we teachers already know the answers. We try and engage students in real responses—explaining their thinking and reactions, and generating their own questions to develop understanding about the novel. Samples of the kinds of response journals we use are explained in chapter 7.

Final Assignments

The final assignment is assigned by the middle of the novel study, so students can be collecting information and working with the end in mind. We try and have these assignments be open-ended enough that all can participate and can stretch themselves in making new connections.

Thanks to teacher, Tina Pali, for contributing the *Tuck Everlasting* assignment.

On the following pages, you will find a sample for the novel *Tuck Everlasting*, called "What? So What?" (page 76) and a sample for *Touching Spirit Bear* that focuses on Drama (page 77).

WHAT? SO WHAT?
Main Assignment for *Tuck Everlasting*

WHAT?
- Carefully choose a combination of five objects, places, and people that are important to the story. (Grade 6 and some ESL students will do three).
- Draw, color, and label each object/place/person.
- Write a quote from the book that relates to that object/place/person, and include the page number.

SO WHAT?
- Tell why each object/place/person is important to the story. Why do you think the author included them in the story? Do they represent something more than meets the eye? An idea? A theme? A value?

CRITERIA
You will earn two marks, Art and Reading.
Art Mark: The five drawings will go toward your ART mark.
- Your drawings are original, colorful, and detailed.
- They complement your quote from the book.

Reading Mark (the written work):
- Your quote from the book matches your drawing.
- Your So What? tells, in your own words, why the object in your illustration is important to the story. This will be approximately 20–25 words.
- Your explanation goes beyond the obvious.
- Your presentation is neat (published on the computer, or neat printing/hand-writing) and has few errors in conventions.

4 Exceeds Expectations	3 Fully Meets Expectations	2+ Generally Meets Expectations	2 Minimally Meets Expectations	1 Not Yet Within Expectations
• All criteria met • Shows depth, original insights, and connections • Completed with extra care and effort • Outstanding	• Strong, confident work • All criteria met • Very good effort • Completed with care	• Capable work • Most criteria met • May be lacking in depth or clarity • May be concerns about presentation or conventions	• Some criteria met • Satisfactory work • No extras • May lack detail and clarity • May be concerns with effort, presentation, or conventions	• Few criteria met • Lack of effort in all areas

Due Date: Your assignment will be due shortly after completion of the novel. However, there will be several draft checks prior to the due date, in order to avoid procrastination!

Parent Signature: _____

DRAMA

Main Assignment for *Touching Spirit Bear*

WHAT?
- Work in groups of 2–6.
- Choose a significant scene from the novel that can be acted out by the number of people in your group.
- Write a script for your scene.
- Practise your script.
- Include props, costumes, and backdrops, as you see fit.
- Be prepared to dramatize your scene for the rest of the class.
- You will have 2 in-class periods to work on this.

CRITERIA

You will be marked on both your script/scene and on your performance.

Script/Scene Mark:
- scene chosen is significant within the novel
- dialogue matches the author's language/character choice and does not stray from the text
- all characters have "speaking" parts (or a pseudo voice for the Spirit Bear)
- script and choice of scene reflect an understanding of the novel

Performance Mark:
- voices are audible
- characters act while "reading" their lines (Your lines do not have to be memorized, but you should be acting, not just reading your lines.)
- the portrayal of the characters is credible
- appropriate use of props and backdrops

4 Exceeds Expectations	3 Fully Meets Expectations	2.5 Generally Meets Expectations	2 Minimally Meets Expectations	1 Not Yet Within Expectations
• All criteria met • Shows insight in interpretation • Writing shows individuality of characters • Creates a mood • All group members skillfully involved	• All criteria met • Well interpreted • Writing matches characters • Attempts to create a mood • All group members involved	• Most criteria met • Shows general understanding of the novel • Writing quite plausible • Captures a moment in the novel • Most group members involved	• Some criteria met • Inaccurate interpretation of the novel • Writing lacks detail, depth • Mostly retelling • Work appears to have been the result of only a few students	• Few criteria met • Lack of understanding of the novel • Undeveloped script or performance • Few students participating

7 Literature Circles: The Basics, the Big Ideas, and Beyond

Keys to Comprehension

Readers who struggle in the middle years frequently struggle with reading comprehension. We have found a surprisingly high percentage of fluent readers in Grades 6 to 9, but also a disappointingly high percentage of readers struggling with comprehension. We believe that this can be improved, but in order to do so, we need to better focus our collective efforts on creating conditions to enable more students to become competent readers.

Richard Allington, President of the International Reading Association, stated (LOMCIRA Fall Conference, 2004) that there are four conditions necessary to support struggling readers:

1. Reading volume
2. High-success reading opportunities
3. Engaging in literate conversations
4. Useful, explicit strategy instruction

We believe that our version of literature circles is an organizational strategy that addresses all of these four conditions. Literature circles provide a seamless format for the resource teacher to move in and out of the classroom, co-teaching and supporting individual students as her schedule permits. It is also easily managed alone by a classroom teacher with a very diverse group of students.

See also Brownlie *Grand Conversations, Thoughtful Responses* (2004), and *Literacy in the Middle Years, Webcast,* Part 2 (2004).

Reading Volume

There are no limits on how much students can read. They are encouraged to read as much as they can in school, and at least 30 minutes a night outside of school. Should a student finish a book overnight, he does not wait for other members of his group to catch up. Instead, he exchanges his book for another. If a student is struggling with reading a book, the classroom teacher or the resource teacher can read with him for a few pages to rekindle interest in the book and build momentum in his reading, and coach him to make personal connections and add to his background knowledge. This can be done without calling a great deal of attention to the student or causing embarrassment, as these book conversations are happening, in some form, as a regular practice in the classroom. The goal is for the students to read and read and read.

High-Success Reading Opportunities

Generally, a collection of six copies each of six different titles (i.e., 36 books) is sufficient for a class of 30.

A collection of books is chosen with the specific students in mind. Within this selection is at least one title that each student in the class *can* read and will *want* to read. The teacher markets the books by telling the students who will like this book, its length and white space, and the kind of time and thinking required to read this book. She also reads an excerpt to give students a feel for the language and tone of the book. Prior to reading the excerpts, the teacher invites the students to imagine themselves reading this book.

Students are reminded that they will meet in groups to discuss these books, but that once they finish their book, they move on to another book and another group. Therefore, students need to choose a book that works for them, not for their friends, as they don't want to be stuck in a book that they didn't really want once their friends have moved on.

Students have free choice in choosing their books—even if they are struggling readers. Generally we give students a day's grace with their books. If, after a day, the student isn't making progress in the book, the teacher can recommend a different book; the reason stated is that the book does not seem to be working for the student, not because the book is too hard. If after two days and some support the student is still not making progress with the chosen title, the teacher asks that the initial book be returned to read at a later date. Student readers are always treated with respect.

More-able readers often choose easier titles, reading them quickly and returning them to the box. This enhances the appeal of these books for struggling readers—to be reading something that others also have read, not just a "special" book for those at risk.

Engaging in Literate Conversations

Too often, struggling readers are assigned meaningless tasks, like comprehension questions or fill-in-the-blank worksheets, that require little or no sophisticated thinking. They come to view reading as matching your thinking with someone else's, and believe that someone else always has a right answer. We do not believe that this is a view of reading appropriate for any student—and it doesn't encourage reading. For students to want to read, they need to see value in reading, and for this they need to be treated as readers. Real readers engage in real conversations with others about the books they read. All readers, struggling or otherwise, need the opportunity to talk with others to deepen their understanding and enrich their experience with the book.

Remember that students in conversation groups are all reading in different parts of the book, so their background knowledge of the book varies widely.

To this end, students meet in groups—one group at a time—with the teacher present. The group is defined by those students who are currently reading a specific book. Group size is best at five or six students; if too few students are currently reading a certain title, invitations can be extended to those who have finished the book to return to the group and join in the conversation. To come to the group, each student has chosen a passage that he/she is willing to read to the rest of the group. Once the passage has been read, each student in the group, including the teacher, "says something" about the passage. If the passage has been stimulating, a free-form discussion will occur once everyone has had a chance to "say something." This free-form discussion is the goal, so sometimes in a group meeting of 15 to 20 minutes, only two students will get to read their passages. If all get to read, that generally signals that the passages did not provoke much discussion.

Expectations for the discussion are simple:

Readers who have read farther or completed the book have one rule: tease and tantalize, but do not spill the beans. The students take this rule seriously.

- Each student will participate and no one student is allowed to dominate.
- The teacher will model good participant behavior, not take over the group.

The groups change as students finish books and move on. Readers who read less quickly—often struggling readers—end up staying with a group for more conversations around the same title. This easy adaptation builds these students' expertise on the particular book and provides them with more time.

The resource teacher can take a group while the classroom teacher takes a different one. While the groups are meeting, the other students read.

"Saying something" about a passage might involve a group member making a connection, asking a question, describing a reaction to the passage when he/she read it, or trying to connect the passage to what he/she is currently reading.

The Say Something strategy is our way of structuring the conversation so that all can participate. It is our replacement for the more traditional assignment of roles. However, it is not an end in itself, and as students' skill with inclusive and impassioned discourse grows, the strategy is set aside for a free-flowing conversation. The same thinking applies to the teacher(s) attending the conversation. Although we love being in the conversation—and the students often prefer us there and invite us back to hear our connections—once the students can handle this conversation independently in a way that includes everyone and enriches understanding, they meet on their own.

Useful, Explicit Strategy Instruction

Strategy instruction occurs with response journals and with comprehension strategies.

Response Journals

Students write in their response journals about three times a week. The purpose of the journal is for students to reflect on their reading and, in so doing, deepen their understanding. We have had the most success with double-entry journals. We use a progression of double-entry formats, folding the page in half and titling the lefthand side "What Happened" and the righthand side "My Thinking."

Left: What Happened	Right: My Thinking
Write 2 events	Write your thinking about each event
OR	
Write 2 quotations	Write your thinking about each quotation

Students begin by writing equal amounts on both sides, but move to writing less on the left side and considerably more on the right.

The teachers model journal writing by writing in front of the students and having them analyze the writing. After several entries, students offer their own journal writing up for analysis. From these samples, criteria are developed to guide subsequent journal writing. Teachers read and respond to most of the journals of younger students, but only weekly to select journals of older students. The teacher's response is descriptive feedback based on co-created criteria; journals are not given a mark. At the end of the literature circles unit, marks are assigned on three journal entries that have been selected by the students.

We also use the double-entry journal as a dialogue journal. In this form, a student writes a letter to a classmate who is currently reading the same book and is in much the same place. The following day, the students exchange their journals and write back to their partners. As with other double-entry journals, the teacher models each phase of the writing: first writing to a partner, then responding in writing to the partner's journal on the following day.

Comprehension Strategies

In middle and secondary grades, teachers and students begin to focus on the techniques the author uses to develop character, plot, and setting.

Every second week, a particular comprehension strategy is taught to all the students. These comprehension strategies often focus on the story elements of setting, character, and plot. Each time a new comprehension strategy is introduced, it is first taught to the whole class, using a novel which they have all read. Based on this teaching, the class establishes the criteria and marking for the strategy assignment. Students then work on their assignment in class, practising the strategy as it has been taught, working with the criteria, and using the novel that they have just completed reading.

Literature Circles within a Term

Building Background Knowledge

Nicole Widdess' Grades 5/6 class is engaged in a thematic unit on slavery. They have been building background knowledge about slavery by reading picture books such as Faith Ringgold's *Aunt Harriet's Underground Railway in the Sky* and *Following the Drinking Gourd* by Janette Winters. With both of these texts, the students have been practising the strategy Quadrants of a Thought (see chapters 1 and 6). Rather than jump right into literature circles, the teacher gently moved from picture books to a whole-class novel. She used the novel to introduce the Say Something strategy and demonstrate how to have a small-group conversation. She then moved to introducing different books to the students for their literature circles, and then on to a research inquiry.

Using a Class Novel to Introduce Literature Circle Conversations

The class novel for Nicole's class is *Rachel: A Mighty Big Imagining* by Lynne Kositsky.

- Ask the class to describe what they think literature circles are.
- Record and post student ideas on a Looks Like/Sounds Like chart.
- Explain that we will practise powerful conversations using a class novel. Later we will move into literature circles with some book choice.
- Preview the novel *Rachel: A Mighty Big Imagining* by Lynne Kositsky.
- Distribute books to the class, one for each two students.
- Read chapter 1 together.
- Assign students to read chapters 2 and 3 with their partners.
- While students are reading, the classroom teacher and the resource teacher each meet with a group of six students and discuss chapter 1 using the Say Something strategy.
- After 15–20 minutes, change groups and discuss with the new groups as much of the text as they have read, using the Say Something strategy.

By dividing the text into two- and three-chapter chunks over the next few days, the teacher can meet with each group once or twice. Each time a meeting is called, the Say Something strategy is used to begin the conversation about the book. After all students have had a chance to respond to the first reading, an open discussion can follow. All students are expected to participate and to come prepared to begin the conversation by reading a quote from the book. Even though not everyone will have a chance to share their quote, everyone will have a chance to speak.

After each group has met at least once, discuss with the class, "What makes a powerful conversation about a book?" Record, categorize, and display the students' ideas.

Literature Circles with Different Books

Nicole, her resource teacher, and her librarian worked together to assemble a thematic text set to provide students book options for literature circles. They chose one non-fiction text and two picture books to include in their set, for use in the same way as the more typical novels. A student with Down Syndrome and four students who were just beginning to learn English as a Second Language were able to have several conversations with the same two picture books as the rest of the students in the class moved through their groups. Progress for two of the ESL students was so rapid that they were able to work with an easier novel by the end of the term. These students were then able to choose any of the books, including the picture books, as their focus for the comprehension activities.

The book choices in the kit included

- *Letters from a Slave Girl*, Mary E. Lyons (more challenging read)
- *Sarny: A Life Remembered*, Gary Paulsen (more challenging read)
- *Jump Ship to Freedom*, JL & C. Collier
- *Jip: His Story*, Katherine Paterson
- *Get on Board: The Story of the Underground Railroad*, Jim Haskens (nonfiction)
- *The Maybe House*, Lynne Kositsky (sequel to *Rachel*, easy read)

Picture book choices for students with special needs and students just beginning to learn English included

- *Barefoot*, Pamela Duncan Edwards
- *O Lord, I Wish I was a Buzzard*, Polly Greenberg

Moving from the Class Novel to the Books in the Text Set

- Introduce each book.
- Remind students to be prepared to choose two books, as they may not get their first book choice.
- Use a chart to keep track of who is reading what book.
- Allow students time to read.
- Meet with students in literature circle groups (each group is reading the same book), calling together one title at a time while the other students continue to read. Use the Say Something strategy to begin the conversation.

Double-Entry Dialogue Journals

- Introduce the concept of the double-entry dialogue journal as letters between friends about the book the two students are reading.
- Model your first entry as a letter on the overhead.
- Encourage students to notice what you are writing, how you keep your audience in mind as you write, how you predict, question, seek clarification, and comment on your surprises.
- Students choose a partner who is reading the same book and is in approximately the same place in the book.
- Students write their first entry.
- The next day, choose one of the students' journal entries. Write a letter on the overhead in response to this student's letter.
- Encourage students to notice how you are responding to what your partner has said, and how you attempt to extend their thinking about the book through your response.
- Students exchange journals and respond to their partner's letter.

Comprehension Strategy: Using Sticky Notes

- Students come to this lesson with a question in mind that they have from the book they are reading.
- Using a piece of text from the class novel, model on the overhead a question that you have. Write the question on a sticky note and place it on the specific part of the text that prompted your question.
- Ask two or three students to demonstrate using a sticky note with a question from their books.
- Encourage students to continue this process independently, finding two or three questions each.
- Students meet in their literature circle groups to discuss their questions.
- Teachers move among the groups, supporting the inquiry.

Moving into Inquiry Groups

Having read several books, Nicole's students began to build a deeper knowledge about issues related to slavery. They used this knowledge to develop meaningful inquiry questions.

Comprehension Strategy: From Quotations to Questions

- Using the class novel model how to use information from the novel to generate questions for further research.
- Using a two-column chart, record a quote from the novel that you have a question about.

Quote	Question

When the question is easy to answer, and can be answered in just a sentence or with a short quote from one of the books, we call this a "thin" question, because we take up very little space to answer it. These questions usually require students to locate a fact.

When a question is more difficult to answer, we call it a "fat" question, because there are many possible explanations and it requires readers to take several quotes or pieces of information to build a reasonable answer.

- Examine the question and ask students to work together in their literature circle groups to find possible answers to the question you have posed.
- Over a week, inquiry groups are asked to record at least five "fat" questions using quotes from their literature circle novels.
- At the end of the week, partners or groups choose one question that they want to research further.

Students may use the other literature circle books or, with support from a teacher, begin to explore other sources to help develop powerful questions and find related information. Many students choose to use the Internet or non-fiction books displayed in the classroom.

Synthesizing Information

The chosen question (from the five fat questions) is the research question. A good research question will generate new questions and help connect information that students have read and are continuing to read.

- Use the chart on page 86 to model how this question will fuel new questions and connect information, using quotes from the class novel.
- Students individually record their information on the chart.
- Students meet with their partners or in groups (those with a common research question) to exchange ideas and record them in their charts.
- This information is used in the final comprehension activity.

Final Comprehension Activity: Drama

The final comprehension activity should pull together all that the students have been learning. It helps with closure, before moving on to another topic. As a final comprehension activity, Nicole chose to have her students create songs and dramatic scenes that demonstrated their understanding of the history of slavery, the impact it has had on individuals' lives, and key themes that their books explored.

Songs

- Discuss with the students what would make a powerful song about the life of a slave; i.e., their criteria.
- Record student thinking. This will be used in a final reflection to comment on the message and impact of one another's songs.
- Students can work individually, in pairs, or in triads.
- Ask students, using their criteria, to create their own songs depicting what they think life for a slave would have been like.
- Remind students to use words that will evoke the feelings of the slaves.
- Students perform their songs.
- Ask students to reflect in writing "How did our songs reflect our criteria?"

Scenes

- Brainstorm with the students scenes to be included in the musical.
- Record ideas on chart paper.

Synthesizing Information

Thinking about...	Related information
Our Question	
New Questions	
Connections	

- Categorize the ideas into big ideas to help create scenes.
- Determine an order for the scenes.
- Have students choose which scene they would like to create.
- Create the scenes and the props in art.

The Production

- Rehearse the whole thing without costumes about five times.
- Have one dress rehearsal.
- Perform for an audience.
- Videotape the performance and watch it together.

8 Poetry: Three Invitations

Changing Our Approach to Poetry

In many classrooms, a "match my thinking" approach to poetry tends to be exclusive.

In many intermediate and middle-school classrooms, poetry is scarcely taught, or it is taught in a very traditional style that relies on the teacher's interpretation of a poem. We want to change this approach to the teaching of poetry. We need to become less apprehensive about the genre, to move beyond a one-right-answer approach, and focus on enjoying and connecting with the poem. In so doing, we include more students and may actually encourage students to read poems independently.

1. Involving Students in Thoughtful Discussion

Each reader brings a unique blend of experiences and background knowledge to reading. These become the lenses for making sense of, or interpreting, a poem. In discussion groups, students share their interpretations, refine their ideas, discover new ways of looking at a poem, and determine which interpretation works best for them. This networking of thinking is both expansive and supportive. It encourages students to read and respond to poetry and to incorporate the precise language of poetry in their oral and written language.

Here is the process we use to involve students in discussions about poetry:

- Read aloud a poem such as "Hiroshima Exit" by Joy Kogawa.
- In heterogeneous groups, students ask each other "I wonder why…" questions about words, phrases, or images from the poem.
- Give a copy of the poem to each student.
- Read the poem aloud again. As they listen, students draw, highlight words and phrases, or jot down ideas and questions around the poem.
- A student volunteer in each group rereads the poem aloud a third time.
- As the students listen, they think about something that they will say about the poem.

"Saying something" might be making a personal connection, telling something the poem reminds a student of, asking a question, identifying something a student would like to know more about.

- Assist students who are learning English and students with communication difficulties with prompts:

    I liked these words in the poem…
    A picture I have in my mind is…
    This poem made me think of…
    I wonder about…

Use student comments to initiate a mini-lesson focusing on some of the poetic devices used in the poem; for example, imagery, repetition, alliteration, metaphor.

- One by one, the students in the group share their ideas and the rest of the students listen and reflect upon the comments.

- Remind students to carefully read again, focusing on the language choice and the poetic devices.
- In groups, students discuss how the poet has used words/phrases in particular ways. Each group tries to reach consensus about what the poet is saying in the poem. The group chooses a spokesperson who explains their interpretation of the poem to the class. Each spokesperson listens carefully so that he/she can build upon or concur with the observations made by the other groups.
- Students complete a five-minute write, contrasting their initial feelings and thoughts about the poem with what they have learned through these discussions.

Evaluation

Throughout this process, the teachers circulate among the groups to provide assistance to those students who are having difficulty expressing their ideas due to shyness, limited English, or special educational needs. The teachers offer suggestions quietly to students who are having difficulty. The class learns to be supportive and wait for these students to explain their ideas. These skills are necessary for all to develop, as there are times when every learner will need the support of a group in order to express him/herself clearly.

This is an excellent opportunity to obtain anecdotal observations reflecting how well students are working within their groups. A checklist can be completed showing each student's ability to communicate positively, take responsibility, contribute to the task, and work cooperatively. To reinforce positive ways of participating in a discussion, teachers can record authentic language used by students in the room. These anonymous responses can later be shared with the class, with the teacher asking students to comment on how successful these responses are in facilitating communication. Searching for and making explicit new and more effective ways to communicate with others is ongoing.

These notes are kept to help form term report card comments on communication and working with others.

2. Three-Dimensional Poetry

One of the many ways to engage students in thinking about poetry is to have them interpret a poem and present their understanding of its meaning in a three-dimensional form. Moving beyond language and discussion allows students with stronger non-verbal skills to show their understanding of a poem. In choosing a way to visually show an audience what a poem is about, students need to become familiar with what they believe the poet is trying to express. The skills they learn in the poetry discussion groups will help the students focus on imagery within the poem, identify poetic devices that the poet has used within the poem, and determine the theme of the poem.

For this project students may choose one of the poems they have written or they may choose a poem from any source, as long as the poet is credited. The task is to think of a way to show the theme or meaning of the poem in a visual way to an audience. A rich and varied selection of poetry should be provided to assist the students in finding a poem that interests them.

This is the process that the students followed to create three dimensional poetry:

For many, the opportunity to construct a concrete representation of a poem is a very motivating experience.

Students end up reading a great variety of poetry during their search to find a suitable poem with a theme that can be represented in a visual format.

We value the opportunity for students to interact and problem solve together as the projects progress.

Project criteria:
• a theme is identified
• a three-dimensional representation that effectively displays the theme is evident
• the theme is supported with text evidence from the poem

Oral presentation criteria:
• voice quality
• expression
• eye contact with audience
• students' own perception of how well their project expresses the poem in terms of its use of materials, format, and representation of the theme

Many thanks to Vancouver teacher and author Jan Wells for her help with the Aberthau sequence, and to Richmond teacher Tina Pali for her help with the Free-Verse Evaluation Sheet.

• Each student selects a poem whose theme or message can be represented visually.
• The criteria for evaluation (see below) is shared with the students.
• Each student decides how to effectively display the poem and the materials that will be used. Examples include mobiles, clay or wood models, origami, dioramas, hand-sewn items, multimedia displays, paintings, found objects.
• Students complete a plan for the design of the representation, including a list of the materials they will use
• Class time is provided so that students can construct their representations within a social context.

Evaluation

Again, using anecdotal comments, information is collected on how well students problem solve during the design process. Students are interviewed individually about how their representation fits the theme or message about the poem that they want to express.

The final component of this assignment is a recitation of the poem for the rest of the class. This requires students to try to commit their poem to memory so that it can be recited confidently. Following the recitation, each student displays his/her three-dimensional representation, tells how it fits the theme of the poem, and explains the aspect of the project that resulted in a personal learning experience.

Both sets of criteria were scored on a four-point scale:

4 Moves beyond all the criteria
3 Meets all the criteria
2 Barely meets the criteria; usually has difficulty in defending the theme
1 Meets few of the criteria

This information is valuable when it comes time to writing the English/ Language Arts portion of the report card for each student. From this activity, we have collected information about comprehension of a poem, information about solving problems, information about students' ability to express themselves both in the physical representation of the poem as well as orally in front of the class, and a personal reflection about their learning.

3. Architectural Tours

All of our communities have unique architecture that is often overlooked in our daily lives. Investigating local architectural design helps students learn about the history of their community. This is highly motivating for students, as it takes them out of the classroom, helps nurture keen powers of observation, and teaches them about building design. These experiences become the catalyst for writing free verse poetry.

Initially, the teacher gathers information about a local historic building. In one case, we studied Aberthau, a house in Vancouver whose name means "a place filled with light." Prior to arriving with the students, we toured the house, made quick sketches of several architectural details in the house, and identified the architects as Samuel MacLure and Cecil Fox. These names then led us to the library to locate books about their architectural style and other buildings in the area.

For the tour with our students, we selected six features of the house to focus upon. In this case, we included the porte-cochère, the stained-glass and mullioned windows, the mock half-timbering, the newel posts, the parquet flooring, and the fireplace in the sitting room. Research was essential so that, when we guided students through the building, each of these features became alive with architectural information and unique stories.

As we planned the tour we considered what questions we could ask the students to enable them to discover why the house was designed as it was. For example, we asked students to consider why the porte-cochère, a covered entry porch for people entering or leaving vehicles, was incorporated as a design feature of the house. This prompted a lively discussion about the kinds of vehicles, mainly horse-drawn carriages, that were the mode of transportation at the time the house was built. The students also noted that the amount of rainfall in Vancouver and the resulting mud made the porte-cochère a must in terms of functional design—a fact that was undoubtedly important to the women of the era, since they wore long gowns!

The lesson proceeded as follows:

- At each of the six focus points, the students listen to a brief overview or a story about the building.
- As they listen, students sketch the architectural feature, and write down notes, personal reflections, or questions about what they see or hear.
- Once the tour is complete, students sit with a partner, look at each other's illustrations, and discuss the features of the building that they found to be most interesting.
- After rereading their notes, students work together to write descriptive phrases from their notes and drawings.
- Students each contribute a description for the teacher to record on the overhead or blackboard.

> Some of the phrases our students contributed:
> "Looking through the old stained glass is like looking back in time"
> "…shimmering, shining Mother of Pearl"
> "…intricate tiled patterns"
> "…a multitude of fireplaces"
> "A rainforest of wood flooring"
> "…damaged by weather and time"
> "Stained glass windows dimmed by renovations"

Students now begin to write a free verse poem about a particular aspect of the house, or about their overall impression of the house. To build this poem, they can use the class phrases, their own phrases, or the information contained in their notes and sketches.

Students who require adaptation of this writing assignment can choose six to ten phrases from the class collection, practise reading them with the teacher or with a partner, choose the order for the phrases, and create a poem.

Using information and unique stories, we helped to build an historical context of the house for the students.

Borrowing ideas from classmates is one of the ways that students learn from others, so that during the writing process, the language starts to become their own.

Evaluation

After several minutes of writing the first draft of their poems, students can share their leads or beginning drafts. Together they work to develop criteria for evaluation. The Free-Verse Evaluation Sheet (page 94) and poems are the work of students in Grades 5 to 7.

> many people
> milling around
> dancing and strutting
> through the party
> I must escape the noise
> I rush up the stairs
> and onto the landing.
> The sun, low in the sky
> shines through the patterned stained glass
> shined oak and polished mahogany
> greet me in my retreat.
>
> *Lea*

> From the window
> in my carriage
> I can see
> the biggest buildings
> When I step in and see
> such beauty
> for a moment I think
> I own the whole thing.
> Then I go through
> the building with care.
>
> *Cam*

Free-Verse Evaluation Sheet

Word Choice

- each word is carefully chosen to create a strong image, using the senses
- more than one of the five senses are used
- language specific to the architecture of the house is used

Student Evaluation   */5*   *Teacher Evaluation*   */5*

Voice

- a personal impression of the house or some aspect of the house is developed

Student Evaluation   */3*   *Teacher Evaluation*   */3*

Flow

- ideas connect together to create an image or an idea

Student Evaluation   */3*   *Teacher Evaluation*   */3*

Ideas and Content

- you stick to your topic
- you help the reader learn about the house and its features

Student Evaluation   */4*   *Teacher Evaluation*   */4*

Givens

- a draft version of your poem will be turned in to the teachers
- a minimum of 6 and a maximum of 20 phrases are included in the poem
- spelling has been checked
- your evaluation sheet has been completed

Student Total: */15*   **Teacher Total:**   */15*

9   An Integrated Unit: Social Studies and English

Time, time, time. How often we hear this lament from teachers working in intermediate and middle-years classrooms. Classroom teachers Fred Weil and Tina Pali work to address this concern. As much as they can, they co-plan. Not only does working together rekindle their energy and spark new ideas, but they find that the collaboration improves their effectiveness as they pool their resources, their talents, and their passions. They work to teach reading and writing within a content area while threading through the content a theme of social responsibility.

Fred and Tina both teach combined Grades 6/7 classes. Their classes are similar to those of many teachers. They teach in an inclusive school where all students are enrolled in the regular classroom. The classes have a high percentage of ESL students, several students on IEPs, a wide range of student ability, and several students for whom behavior is an issue. All students are expected to participate and learn in this project. They are supported in their learning as much as possible, although in-class resource support was not available at the time of this unit.

Curriculum Content

The social studies content is an examination and understanding of children's rights in different parts of the world. This content is uncovered by reading and responding to a variety of novels on the theme of children's rights, considering especially the following aspects of social responsibility:

- contributing to the classroom and the community
- solving problems in peaceful ways
- valuing diversity and defending human rights
- exercising democratic rights and responsibilities.

To prepare, Fred and Tina read a wide selection of novels that connected to the theme of children's rights and that would address the range of reading abilities in their classes. They also chose a variety of picture books that connected to the theme and would be used to model each assignment and to build background knowledge. These books would be available for all students to reread, but prove especially pertinent for several significantly less-able readers, who found many of the novels challenging. A new open-ended assignment was modeled each week of the project.

Bibliography

Easier

Kidd, Diana. *Onion Tears*. New York: Harper Trophy, 1993

Laird, Elizabeth. *Secret Friends*. London: Hodder Children's Books, 1996

Lowry, Lois. *Number the Stars*. New York: Yearling, 1990

Martin, Ann. *Belle Teal*. New York: Scholastic, 2005

Naidoo, Beverley. *Journey to Jo'burg*. New York: Harper Trophy, 1988

Whelan, Gloria. *Goodbye Vietnam*. New York: Knopf, 1992

Girls' Preferences

Ellis, Deborah. *The Heaven Shop*. Markham: Fitzhenry and Whiteside, 2004

Filipovic, Zlata. *Zlata's Diary*. New York: Penguin, 1995

Nye, Naomi Shihab. *Habibi*. New York: Simon Pulse, 1999

Sterling, Shirley. *My Name is Seepeetza*. Vancouver: Douglas & McIntyre, 1992

Whelan, Gloria. *Homeless Bird*. New York: Harper Trophy, 2001

Yolen, Jane. *Devil's Arithmetic*. New York: Puffin, 1990

Boys' Preferences

D'Adamo, Francesco. *Iqbal*. New York: Atheneum Books for Young Readers, 2001

Ho, Minfong. *The Clay Marble*. New York: Farrar, Straus and Giroux, 2003

Pearson, Kit. *Awake and Dreaming*. Toronto: Penguin, 1997

Watkins, Yoko Kawashima. *So Far From the Bamboo Grove*. New York: Lothrop, Lee and Shepard, 1986

Watkins, Yoko Kawashima. *My Brother, My Sister and I*. (sequel) New York: Simon Pulse, 1996

Williams, Laura. *Behind the Bedroom Wall*. Minneapolis, MN: Milkweed, 1996

Good Reads

Ellis, Deborah. *The Breadwinner*. Toronto: Groundwood Books, 2001

Ellis, Deborah. *Parvana's Journey*. (sequel) Toronto: Groundwood Books, 2003

Ellis, Deborah. *Mud City*. (sequel) Toronto: Groundwood Books, 2004

Haddix, Margaret Peterson. *Among the Hidden (Shadow Children #1)*. New York: Aladdin, 2000

Laird, Elizabeth. *The Garbage King*. London: Macmillan Children's Books, 2003

Macken, Walter. *Flight of the Doves*. London: Macmillan Children's Books, 2001

Mikaelsen, Ben. *Petey*. New York: Hyperion, 1998

Naidoo, Beverley. *No Turning Back*. New York: Harper Trophy, 1999

Palermo, Sharon. *The Lie That Had To Be*. Saskatoon, SK: Thistledown Press, 1995

Park, Linda Sue. *A Single Shard*. New York: Yearling, 2001

Picture Books

Aliki. *Painted Words, Spoken Memories*. New York: Greenwillow, 1998

Bradby, Marie. *More Than Anything Else*. New York: Orchard, 1995

Cutler, Jane. *The Cello of Mr. O*. New York: Dutton Children's Books, 1999

Heide, Florence Parry & Judith Heide Gilliland. *Sami and the Time of the Troubles*. New York: Clarion Books, 1992

Kaplan, William. *One More Border*. Vancouver: Douglas & McIntyre, 1998

Zhang, Ange. *Red Land Yellow River*. Vancouver: Douglas & McIntyre, 2004

Beginning

Fred and Tina assigned students to pairs or groups of three, based roughly on their reading ability and on their ability to work well as partners or groups. These partners/groups stayed together for the three- to four-week period, and agree to read at roughly the same pace. The teachers quickly introduced the novels (available in twos and threes) to the students, and invited them to choose the one they and their partner(s) wanted to begin reading.

These teachers believe in clear expectations. They also believe in involving parents as partners in the shared enterprise of their children's learning, so a unit overview is sent home and signed by the parents (see below). Students are expected to read at least 30 minutes a night.

> End-of-the-unit reflections suggested the students would have preferred a partner change during the month and that, in choosing partners, teachers should have paid more attention as to what sports teams were currently eating up a lot of certain students' time!

Children's Rights Literature Project

Time Period: October 14th – November 14th

Mr. Weil and Mrs. Pali have selected numerous books for you to choose from. We are both avid readers of children's literature and, believe it or not, have read all of them (lucky you!) We have also carefully chosen a reading partner for you. Due to uneven numbers there are a few triads. All of the books have a common theme connecting to Children's Rights, which we are learning about in Social Studies this term. Many of you will read 5 or 6 books easily, some may read 3. The most important thing is that you are meeting your responsibilities and putting your best effort into your assignments.

Your Responsibilities:
- Read a minimum of 30 minutes each night (including weekends). You should read more if there is no additional homework that night. We expect you to come to a consensus with your partner, as to the amount you will read.
- Be prepared for, and contribute to, partner and class discussions.
- Use the time given during class for reading, writing responses, and assignments wisely.
- Be cooperative with your partner, i.e., don't let others down by not doing the reading and coming to class unprepared.

Assignments
- You will be submitting small weekly assignments (e.g., double-sided response entries). More details of these will be given in class.

The Marks You Earn Will Be Based On
- the degree to which you meet the given criteria for your assignments
- your participation in partner and class discussions
- your demonstration of responsibility to yourself and your partner (being focused, cooperative, prepared)

Although we trust you and know you are responsible and cooperative, please approach your teacher if you need help in problem solving with your partner.

Please explain your responsibilities to your parents, who will sign below. Happy reading!

Mrs. Pali and Mr. Weil

Each Week

A pattern emerged each week.

Monday

A picture book connecting to the theme was read. The new assignment was introduced. Criteria were established for the assignment. The teachers modeled how to complete the assignment, using the text from the picture book. The class, using the criteria, discussed how to edit the teacher's work to best achieve the criteria.

Tuesday/Wednesday

An atlas was always available in the class, and teachers began to collect background pictures to establish a context for the settings of the various novels.

Students read their books, alone or with their partner(s), and each worked on completing a draft of the assignment. These were handed in on Wednesday for feedback from the teachers. While the students worked, the teachers moved around the class, interacting with the pairs and triads of readers, monitoring their progress, reading with them, checking their understanding, scaffolding their growing understanding. One of the important tasks of the teachers was to help provide historical background for the novels.

Thursday

As the assignments were returned to the students, the teachers taught a mini-lesson on whatever need was most evident in the drafts of the students' assignments. Because the books were so compelling and this feedback was so pertinent, the class discussion at this point was highly engaging. Students were animated and involved, discussing their books and the challenges that their characters were encountering. As time permitted, students continued to read.

Friday

Students discussed, in small groups or as a class, their assignment in terms of the book they were reading, and handed the assignment in for evaluation. As time permitted, they read.

There are several factors key to the success of this kind of teaching:

- The curriculum is engaging and issue-based.
- There is choice for students.
- All students have texts available to them that they *can* read and will *want* to read.
- Students can read at their own pace and are not racing to keep up with the class or being held back by the class.
- All students have the opportunity to engage in literate conversations with their peers.
- There is ample time for, and an expectation of, large amounts of reading.
- Teachers model the desired student performance, provide explicit criteria for meeting the expected performance, coach and give direct feedback during the working of the assignment, and only give a mark after much learning and practising has occurred.

- Student talk abounds in the classroom.
- There are high expectations for all students, and support provided as needed for all to meet these expectations. Adaptations easily occur within the context of the regular classroom and the regular curriculum.
- Students do not flounder within a long-term assignment. There is a mandatory midweek check-up, and teachers can additionally monitor those students who have difficulty organizing their time.

Sample Assignments

There are five assignments presented here. Typically, the teachers choose three or four of them.

Assignment #1: Significant Events

An event in a story is significant when it changes the main character's life, his/her growth as a person, and/or his/her relationship with another character. The character may make a decision that has a dramatic impact on his/her life. Remember, for this assignment, an event is not a situation, such as war or poverty, but rather something specific that causes the character to grow and change. Think about the examples we have discussed in class.

Due Date

8:45 a.m. Thursday

What You Have to Do

Choose three events in your story that you think are the most significant, and explain why. Each explanation will be no longer than one paragraph. Of course, you must retell some of the story to explain your event, but we are looking for your thinking, not just retelling.

Criteria for each Paragraph

- knowledge of the story is demonstrated by the chosen event
- strong justification for choice of event
- writing flows smoothly and makes sense
- use of sophisticated language

Format

Use the paper size you need to show the events and paragraphs. One, and only one, of your events will be illustrated in the form of a cartoon: with two or three panels and thinking and/or talking bubbles, show what is important to the character(s) in the situation. You still will need a paragraph to go with the cartoon.

How You Will Earn Your Mark

Paragraphs: 5 marks each; total of 15 marks
Cartoon: 3 marks
Overall Presentation, Neatness, Conventions: 3 marks

Other

- Naturally, you will talk with your partner about significant events, but this is an individual project and we do not expect your projects to be the same.
- You will be required to have your drafts at school for us to check your progress on Tuesday.
- Some students will be doing an adapted assignment and will be approached individually by their teachers.
- ESL students are expected to ask for help with grammar before the due date.

~Petey~   By Nicole

1) Petey meets Calvin pg.43

I think that is important because Petey becomes (and has) a friend. Petey finally has someone to talk (well at least attempt) to and relate to. Calvin plays a important role in Petey's life, a friend a brother, and family. They spend all there time together and Calvin is the only one who can understand Petey's "Aaoo's" and "Aaee's," the only one who tries to figure out what's going on in Petey's mind, the only one to be his friend.

2) Petey meets Trevor (Trevor sticks up for Petey) pg.147

When Trevor sees three boys picking on an old man (Petey) he sticks up for him and tries to tell the boys to "knock it off!" It seems to me that Trevor was unsure of what he was doing and thought twice before making a difference. Trevor was taking a big risk, he knew the boys would think differently about him, but that's what Petey likes about him, his courage and his friendliness.

3) Petey becomes a Grandfather pg.277

It really touches me when Trevor asks Petey to be his Grandfather. I think it meant a lot to Petey because he was very ill at the time and for someone so young to understand him, takes courage, care and understanding. I think Trevor is very mature for his age, befriending a crippled old man would be overwhelming and almost "scary" for someone so young. Petey must of felt so loved when Trevor proposed the question "Will you be my Grandfather?" Petey must feel like a real "Grandpa."

Assignment #2: Rights of the Child

The Ten Rights of the Child according to the United Nations are listed on your information sheet (see The Ten Rights on page 102). These are rights that this group of nations agree that all children should have. In your novel, your character(s) will be denied some of these rights. As you and your partner are reading, search for evidence of what rights are being denied.

Due Date

8:45 a.m. Friday

What You Have to Do

Choose three of the children's rights which your character does not have. For each right, give specific evidence from your novel that proves that he/she is being denied that right.

Criteria

- at least three examples of denied children's rights
- specific evidence from the story that demonstrates how the right is denied
- information presented in a clear, organized, and interesting way

Format

- use 8.5" × 11" paper
- choose any format you wish, provided you meet the criteria

How You Will Earn Your Mark

Rights and evidence: detailed evidence from the story to show the character has at least three children's rights denied: 10 marks
Presentation: organized, categorized presentation of information: 3 marks
Conventions: few errors, which do not interfere with meaning: 2 marks

Other

- Naturally, you will talk with your partner about denied Children's Rights and supporting evidence, but this is an individual project and we do not expect your projects to be the same.
- You will be required to have your drafts at school for us to check your progress on Wednesday.
- Some students will be doing an adapted assignment and will be approached individually by their teachers to make a plan.
- ESL students are expected to ask for help with grammar before the due date.

The Ten Rights

1. **EDUCATION**—our right to an education
We have the right to education. Governments have the responsibility to guarantee that primary education is compulsory and free of charge, and to take steps so that we all have equal access to secondary and higher education. The discipline used in our schools must not go against our human dignity. Our education must develop our own personalities and abilities; prepare us to become a responsible member of a free society; develop respect for our parents or guardians, for human rights, for the environment, and for the cultural and national values of ourselves and others.

2. **FAMILY**—our right to have family to care for us
We have the right to live with our parents unless this is against our best interests, and to be reunited with our families across international borders. Both of our parents are responsible for our upbringing; governments must respect this and support our parents in bringing us up. Our right to care also means that if we are deprived of a family environment we have the right to special protection, are entitled to alternative care that respects our background, and have the right to a regular review of that care. In the case of adoption, our best interests must be considered.

3. **FOOD & SHELTER**—our right to food and shelter
We have the right to a decent standard of living for our physical, mental, spiritual, moral, and social well-being and we have the right to benefit from social security, including social insurance. Those of us who have a disability have the right to special care, education, and training.

4. **HEALTH**—our right to a safe environment and healthy life
Governments must do everything possible to make sure children survive and develop. We have the right to the best possible level of health care available, to clean air and water.

5. **NAME & NATIONALITY**—our right to have a name and acquire a nationality
We have the right to be given a name, to acquire a nationality and, whenever possible, to know and to be cared for by our parents. Governments have an obligation to protect our identity, name, nationality, and family ties.

6. **NON-DISCRIMINATION**—our right to be treated fairly without discrimination
All rights apply to all children, no matter who we are or where we live.

7. **OWN CULTURE**—our right to our own cultures
We have the right to enjoy and practise our own cultures, languages, and religions, especially if we belong to a minority or indigenous population.

8. **PROTECTION FROM HARM**—our right to protection from harmful acts
We have the right to be protected from abuse, neglect, torture, sexual exploitation, the use and distribution of drugs, and abduction. We have the right to be protected from having to participate in work that threatens our health, education, or development. We have the right to special protection in times of war and fair treatment if arrested. Governments must take steps to prevent harm and exploitation and to provide treatment for those who have been abused or exploited, have been in conflict with the law, or have experienced armed conflict or torture. Governments must set minimum ages for employment and regulate working conditions.

9. **REST & PLAY**—our right to rest and play
We have the right to rest, leisure, play, and participation in cultural and artistic activities.

10. **SHARE OPINIONS**—our right to share our opinions
We have the right to express our views and opinions and to have these opinions listened to in matters that affect us. We have the right to freedom of thought, conscience, and religion, the freedom to receive information from many sources, the freedom to meet with others and to join or start our own associations, and the freedom from governmental invasions of our privacy.

My Name Is Seepeetza

Seepeetza didn't have
The Right to her Own Culture
It was in the law that the Indians couldn't practice their own religion. The nuns taught them in school and made them practice the Catholic religion. The Indian children had to learn English; some of them even forgot how to speak their native language. The nuns also had them change their Indian names to Catholic names.

Seepeetza didn't have
The Right to Protection from Harm
The nuns used the strap and other awful devices for discipline. It doesn't do anything except make all the kids that get beat, dislike the nuns and wish that they didn't have to go to that school.

Seepeetza didn't have
The Right of Non Discrimination
She was discriminated against for being an Indian. She had to change her Indian name to a Catholic name, which was Martha. She was not allowed to be taught by Indians, but was forced to travel far away to learn the Catholic ways instead of her Indian traditions. I think the nuns should treat Indians like they treat themselves, because the Indians are people just like the nuns, the only thing that is different between them is their race, and that should have nothing to do with whether or not they like each other.

By Clint

Assignment #3: Double-Entry Response Journals

There are ten different double-entry response journal prompts. Essentially, the question on the lefthand side of the page will require you to think specifically about text-based information. The question on the righthand side of the page will require you to use this text information to think critically, make inferences, respond personally, or offer supported reactions and opinions.

Due Date

8:45 a.m. Friday

What You Have to Do

Choose four of the ten response journal prompts that will best demonstrate your understanding of the novel. Assume that to respond well to each response prompt on the righthand side of the page will take a considerable amount of writing, likely about a page.

Criteria/Marks

- lefthand questions: 4 well-chosen and accurately documented responses (with specific text references): 2 marks each; total of 8 marks
- righthand questions: sophisticated responses containing personal connections (between books or between the book and your life), supported reactions and opinions, inferential thinking and/or critical thinking: 4 marks each; total of 16 marks
- writing: connected thoughts, sophisticated language: 3 marks
- conventions: errors in spelling and grammar do not interfere with meaning: 2 marks

Ten Double-Entry Journal Response Prompts

1. What is the setting of your novel?	1. Describe the setting of the novel in terms of things like landscape, climate, time period, human environment, etc. How does the main character fit into the setting? How does it compare with where you live?
2. What question do you have from reading this novel?	2. Ask your question to at least 2 different people. What do you learn from their responses?
3. Find a passage that is very descriptive. Write this out and sketch your image of the passage.	3. How does the author create the image of a particular setting, character, or event in this passage? Does the author use imagery or special language?
4. What is an important choice or decision that a character has to make?	4. Explain the choice, why the character makes it, and whether you think it was a wise choice.
5. What is an important relationship that a main character has with another character?	5. Explain who the relationship is with and what kind of relationship it is. Explain how the relationship develops or changes over time.
6. What inner resources does the main character use to overcome the challenges that he or she faces?	6. Explain what character traits and personal strengths the main character has and give specific examples from the story of when he/she demonstrates these traits.
7. How does a main character show personal growth or change over the course of the story?	7. Explain how the character experiences a change in their personality that is positive, such as greater resilience, understanding, or caring for others.
8. Is there an artifact or object that has special significance in your story?	8. Explain why a particular object is important in the story. Does the author use that object as a symbol of some kind?
9. What is the meaning of the title?	9. Explain the title of the story. You might comment on whether you think it is well chosen or not. Would you have chosen a different title for the story?
10. Choose an event that you found particularly frightening or hopeful. Retell this event.	10. Explain why the event was particularly frightening or hopeful to you. Be sure to make personal connections and support your opinion with specific detail.

Assignment #4: Triple Venn Diagram

A Venn Diagram is a graphic organizer that helps organize your thinking while you compare and contrast three characters from three different books you have read.

Due Date

8:45 a.m. Thursday

What You Have to Do

Compare and contrast three characters from the three books you have read in the form of a Venn Diagram. Describe, in point form, similarities and differences between your three characters. If you have read only two books, you can be the third character. Use the areas where the circles overlap to show similarities, and the rest of the circle to show differences.

Criteria

- important character traits
- family information
- the setting/situation your character is in (e.g., Germany in WW II)
- the children's rights your character is being denied
- any other information that is relevant to your novel

Format

- label each circle with your character and the novel title
- use an 11" × 14" or 11" × 17" piece of paper so you have lots of room for neat printing
- if you are able to do Venn Diagrams on your computer, go for it!

How You Will Earn Your Mark

- Selecting a range of important similarities and differences in your characters on the basis of
  - character traits
  - family information
  - setting/situation
  - children's rights that are being denied
  - other information relevant to your novel

15 possible marks

- Overall presentation including
  - conventions such as spelling and capitalization
  - neatness
  - use of titles and headings
  - design and illustrations that are related to your novels

5 possible marks

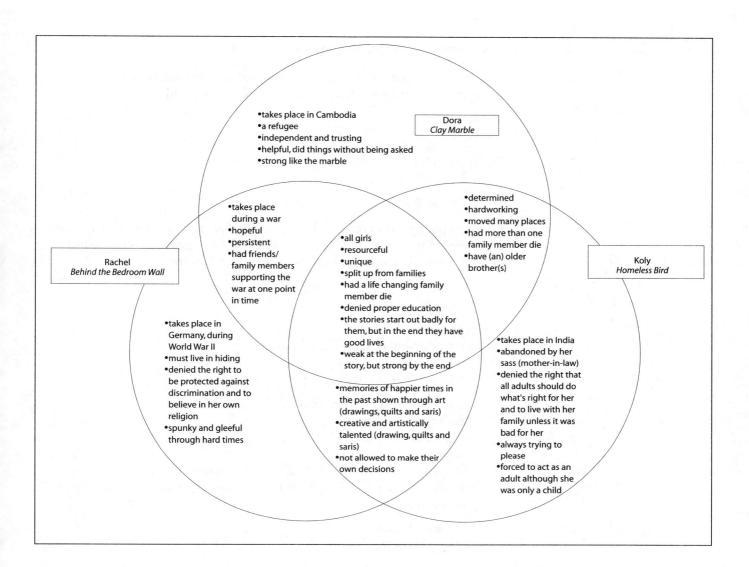

Dora
Clay Marble

- takes place in Cambodia
- a refugee
- independent and trusting
- helpful, did things without being asked
- strong like the marble

- determined
- hardworking
- moved many places
- had more than one family member die
- have (an) older brother(s)

Rachel
Behind the Bedroom Wall

Koly
Homeless Bird

- takes place during a war
- hopeful
- persistent
- had friends/ family members supporting the war at one point in time

- all girls
- resourceful
- unique
- split up from families
- had a life changing family member die
- denied proper education
- the stories start out badly for them, but in the end they have good lives
- weak at the beginning of the story, but strong by the end

- takes place in Germany, during World War II
- must live in hiding
- denied the right to be protected against discrimination and to believe in her own religion
- spunky and gleeful through hard times

- memories of happier times in the past shown through art (drawings, quilts and saris)
- creative and artistically talented (drawing, quilts and saris)
- not allowed to make their own decisions

- takes place in India
- abandoned by her sass (mother-in-law)
- denied the right that all adults should do what's right for her and to live with her family unless it was bad for her
- always trying to please
- forced to act as an adult although she was only a child

Assignment #5: Readers Theatre

Readers theatre is an opportunity for you and your partner to represent and share an important event from a book you have both read.

Due Date

Friday, class time

What You Have to Do

Choose a passage from the novel with a lot of dialogue, or a particularly significant event in the novel, and create a dialogue for it. Together you and your partner will write the dialogue, then present it to the class.

Criteria/Marks

- Script
  - introduction to the passage, 3 marks
  - script choice, 2 marks
  - script content, 3 marks

- Performance (for each presenter)
  - volume, 4 marks
  - expression, 4 marks
  - stayed in role, 2 marks
- Peer and self-evaluation: How did you and your partner(s) contribute to this activity? Make a circle graph to show your contributions and explain your thinking.

> Readers Theatre
> Flight of the Doves
>
> Judge, Derval – Chase
> Finn, Narrator, Uncle Toby – Gerry
>
> Introduction: Our story is called "Flight of the Doves" and it takes place in England and Ireland. Finn and Derval are brother and sister at ages 12 and 7. Finn and Derval wanted to escape their vicious uncle Toby and went to Ireland where their loving granny and uncle RC and uncle Paddy live. They make it to their destination but they also had many cops and citizens trying to get them back to uncle Toby. We picked the scene where Finn and Derval were in granny's house and they are being questioned by the judge. Suddenly, Derval says something shocking and the judge tries to find the truth. We picked this scene because it really was powerful, the way Derval had the courage to speak up the truth and say such a thing.
>
> JUDGE: Do you feel that you have done a great deed, running away from home, crossing the sea, making hares out of police, and triumphantly arriving at your destination?
> FINN: Oh no.
> JUDGE: But you should, it was a remarkable thing to do.
> FINN: But I didn't do it.
> JUDGE: What do you mean?

FINN: Well, it was all the other people, all the people that helped us. Poll, Tom, Mickser, Moses and Michael. If it wasn't for them we would have been caught long ago.

JUDGE: I see. So you hadn't much to do with it.

FINN: Oh no.

JUDGE: I see. If you are returned to your uncle Toby, what would you do, Finn?

FINN: I would run away the first chance I got.

JUDGE: Would you bring Derval?

FINN: Yes.

JUDGE: Why?

10 Science/Ecology: Working with the Eight Intelligences

Broadening the Means of Scientific Communication

In seeking a framework to broaden the means by which scientific knowledge could be communicated, we utilized Howard Gardner's theory of multiple intelligences (Fogarty, 1997).

When co-planning the Ecology component of the Life Sciences strand in the Grades 6 and 7 science curriculum, the resource teacher and teacher librarian worked with me (the classroom teacher) to enhance our students' ability to communicate scientifically. The activities in this unit were designed to allow students to build their knowledge and then demonstrate it in a variety of ways. Students learning English as a second language can build their understanding through a variety of experiences, not just reading and writing. Students who thrive on open-ended exploration have no ceiling placed on their participation. Students who experience academic difficulties can prove to be very powerful learners when provided with new ways to demonstrate their understanding.

In multiple-intelligence theory, there are eight ways of learning. These intelligences are

- verbal-linguistic
- logical-mathematical
- visual-spatial
- musical
- bodily-kinesthetic
- naturalist
- interpersonal
- intrapersonal

Building Background Information

The concepts we chose to teach in this unit included the following terms: *herbivore, omnivore, carnivore, decomposer, food web, food chain, ecosystem, biogeoclimatic zone, predator, prey, biodiversity, interdependent, life cycle, producer, consumer, photosynthesis.*

During our planning it became clear that, to reach the goal of teaching students to communicate scientifically, we needed to provide opportunities for the students to develop a repertoire of skills that enabled them to integrate these intelligences.

We designed a variety of lessons that involved students in discovering more about the important concepts through small group activities:

See also People Search on pages 14–16.

- a People Hunt at the beginning of the unit to determine the level of understanding that the students possessed about these ecological concepts (see People Hunt on page 112)
- making three-column notes (see Three-Column Notes on page 113) when watching a video or reading non-fiction texts; students then worked together to ensure that each group member had accurately recorded facts, details, and drawings for each of the concepts

People Hunt

Directions

Meet for short periods of time with your classmates so you can learn more about the following concepts. As you gather information, record the answer and ask the student to sign his/her name in corresponding box. Each box must contain the name of a different student.

Find someone who:

Knows the name of a carnivore from a famous movie or fairy tale	Can explain what the prefix *bio* means	Can make a sketch of a local ecosystem
_____	_____	_____
Signature	Signature	Signature
Knows some of the things that a herbivore would eat	Can name a decomposer that is eaten in salads	Can explain why photosynthesis is important
_____	_____	_____
Signature	Signature	Signature
Can draw and label a predator as it stalks its prey	Can name a famous omnivore living in BC forests	Is able to guess what a Biogeoclimatic zone is
_____	_____	_____
Signature	Signature	Signature

Three-Column Notes

Word and its meaning	Details	Drawing
1.	a. b. c.	
2.	a. b. c.	
3.	a. b. c.	
4.	a. b. c.	
5.	a. b. c.	

- making personal connections, text/media connections, and connections to the world around them when students discussed these concepts in small and large groups (see Making Connections on page 115)
- showing a food web or life cycle using movement or drama and music
- obtaining information through multi-source and multi-level resources, including picture books, magazines, non-fiction books, pamphlets, video, and websites; for students in Grades 6/7, the selection of books included those read by students in Grades 4 though 8.

Once the students had gained an understanding of these concepts, a field trip was planned to develop the students' observational skills and their naturalist and bodily-kinesthetic intelligences in a forest setting. Park naturalists designed the outdoor activities so that these concepts would come alive for the students. The naturalists reinforced the vocabulary that had been used throughout the unit, demonstrating to the students how biologists used these concepts when communicating with others.

Evaluation: Multiple Representations of Understanding

We wanted to assess how well the team worked together to achieve their goal of communicating in a scientific way, and we also wanted to know how well individual students could communicate their knowledge.

To deepen the students' understanding, we designed our summative assessment so that they could make connections between the concepts taught in the unit and a local ecosystem. The evaluation had to be both group and individual.

Here are the steps we followed:

1. Students were placed in heterogeneous groups. From a list of local ecosystems—seashore, pond, estuary, river, forest, marsh, or creek—each group chose one for their project.

2. The students arranged a field study so that they could visit the ecosystem together. Observations of the area were made in a variety of ways including life lists, photographs, video recordings, observational notes, and drawings

3. Each student in the group would become an expert by learning in-depth about one organism in the ecosystem. A two-page essay was written by each student (following the Essay Outline on page 116) about his/her chosen organism.

4. The art teacher showed students techniques for constructing a diorama.

5. Each group constructed a diorama, using non-living materials to show the insects, birds, plants, reptiles, and animals living in the ecosystem. The diorama had to include the organisms researched by each group member and also a clearly labeled food web.

Evaluation of the essays and dioramas was completed using the following process:

- The students brainstormed all the important components of the dioramas and of the essays.
- The teachers helped the students to organize the criteria into categories for ease of evaluation. If needed, we added criteria and explained to the students why these were important to include.

Making Connections

Topic _____

Things I know and things about me	Other things I've read, watched in movies, or seen on TV	Connections to the world and big ideas

Essay Outline: Interdependence Project

Use the following format as a guide for the essay about the organism you chose for your part of the Interdependence Project.

Paragraph 1

- topic sentence that introduces the essay subject
- identify the organism that has been studied
- include the Latin and common names (if both can be found)
- tell whether your organism is a predator or prey

Paragraph 2

- location of the organism
- describe the ecosystem, niche, climate, and biogeoclimatic zone where your organism lives and finds shelter
- describe the other organisms that live in this ecosystem

Paragraph 3

- explain how the organism fits into the Food Web
- describe and provide evidence of the organism as a herbivore, carnivore, or omnivore
- explain how the organism is interdependent with other organisms

Paragraph 4

- describe changes in the ecosystem that have occurred or are still occurring
- describe problems which this organism has to face
- describe the adaptations, if any, the organism has made to survive

Paragraph 5

- summarize the main ideas of your essay
- describe what needs to be done to protect this organism
- describe what must be done to protect the ecosystem where it lives
- leave the readers with an idea of something that they could do to assist in protecting the biodiversity in our local ecosystems

Bibliography

Please include all of the resources you used and follow the bibliography format outlined by the Teacher Librarian.

Essay components included
- accurate use of scientific vocabulary
- bibliography format used consistently
- all paragraph subtopics included
- conventions of writing.

Diorama components included
- realistic representation of the ecosystem
- food web clearly shown
- overall impact of the diorama
- organisms represented in the diorama.

Throughout this process, students were able to read and see the projects produced by other students in the class. When they saw the range of ways to complete the project, they gained new ideas for tackling future assignments.

- The criteria and rating scale were posted and the teams polished their dioramas against these criteria before moving to the team evaluation process.
- During the team evaluation process, students continued to work in the same groups. Each group was given a different component of the project to evaluate.
- Each group worked together to arrive at a consensus before assigning a score out of 5 for the project component they were evaluating.
- The teachers reviewed the marks assigned by the student teams.
- The essays were read by the teachers and evaluated using the following scale:

    5 The student has exceeded the expectations, demonstrating insight and creativity.
    4 The student has successfully met all of the criteria.
    3 The student has met most of the criteria.
    2 The student has met only some of the criteria.
    1 The task was inappropriate for the student at this time.

The evaluation process gave students a chance to witness how a subjective evaluation is completed. Some of the groups' debates on how to score particular projects were very illuminating for us as teachers. In most cases, it was evident that the students valued the same things that we did when evaluating their work. The students had fun, experienced a great deal of success, learned a lot of science, and moved their learning outside the traditional boundaries of the classroom. The following two essays are samples of how all students could participate with success in this unit.

Raccoon   By: Lindsay

Have you ever shooed away a raccoon eating your garbage? Next time that you see one, stop and watch it for awhile. You will see that raccoons are very misunderstood. Raccoons are very playful creatures and they are not trying to upset humans. The fact that they have adapted to city life and are not afraid of humans is not their fault at all. Raccoons are consumers. They eat other things. So why are they living in the center of the city? This and much more will be answered in this report.

The raccoon is an omnivore. This means they eat a variety of different things. Some of the raccoons favorite foods are: crayfish, fish, frogs, garbage, mice and squirrels. The raccoon also eats things that are already dead and some plants. Because most things raccoons eat live in the water, they like to live where there is fresh water nearby. There is not a lot of things that eat raccoons but since they live near the city, the raccoon population is kept down by people in cars and the fact that they are not protected. Some things that do eat raccoons are cougars, bears, wolves and other big cats. Most of these animals prefer to eat the babies.

The raccoon lives in the forest. They live in cavities in trees, ditches in the ground and other sheltered areas. Raccoons are not very picky about their location but since they like to live near water, they usually don't live very high up in the mountains. They also can't survive in very, very cold climates like the Yukon. Most raccoons don't care about what kind of forests they live in as long as they have all of the above. This is probably why they like Vancouver so much. The fact is, they are not living in the city, we are living in the forest. If you think about it, raccoons have probably been living in Vancouver for hundreds of years. Then we decided to build our city right in the middle of the forest. For example, the North shore mountains, Stanley

Park and Pacific Spirit Park were all here before us and were all homes for raccoons. Now raccoons have decided to live in city parks because we took down so much of their habitat.

A raccoon's life cycle is very simple. They are considered babies for around two years. For the first year, they stay in their homes almost all of the time. They live on their mothers' milk for only about six months. When they are two years old, they can leave their homes but they usually stay close to their mothers for the first month. Baby raccoons are very playful and curious. This is how most baby raccoons are hurt or killed. They sometimes might wander on to a busy road without their mothers seeing and end up badly injured. Raccoons in zoos can live up to about fifteen years but in the wild they live about only twelve years because of the amount of dangers.

Some drastic changes that have happened in the raccoons ecosystem are clear cutting, highways and toxic garbage. Raccoons are now used to traffic and people but they don't always remember about cars when they are crossing the road. They have become so used to roads being there that they don't consider them being a threat. One major change to the ecosystem is that the forest is being cut down rapidly. This is why raccoons are not living in parks, riverbeds and even people's backyards. Another threat to raccoons is that if people throw away some fish and toxic garbage in the same bag, the raccoons might eat the poison and get sick or die.

So next time you see a raccoon, watch it and learn. Try to be careful not to throw away toxins and food in the same bag and learn to care about the forest. We protect our homes from burglars but raccoons can't protect the forest against us.

Cat Tails   Byron

The cat tail has two names—one is called a cat tail and the other name is bull rush. Some people and a lot of books call it a cat tail because at the end of the brown round part it looks like it has a tail. The cat tails have flat leaves abut an inch wide. They have a strong stem that grows high. Four quarters of the way up is a dark brown and oval shape, which is part of the cat tail. The cat tail contains pollen grains and just above it is a little tip that looks like a tail. The Latin name for cat tails is Typha Latifotia. This organism is prey for the Red Wing Black birds and the Muskrats.

This organism is located in estuaries in Vancouver and Richmond and many other places. I saw them in Terra Nova next to the river – there are thousands of them growing there. Cat tails live in many different climates including those which get snow to heat. It lives in very swampy waters, but has no shelter from rain. A lot of dead trees are in the area where they live.

The cat tails fit into the food web when Red Wing Black birds or Muskrats take the pollen for food. Then they die over the years and make better soil which the cat tails use to survive. When the snow geese come near winter they drop their droppings and that is good for the soil too. Cat tails are eaten by Herbivores because they use the soil to survive. If there was no soil or animals there would not be any cat tails.

There is less room for them to grow because people took up all the room in the beginning of Terra Nova and in other places. It is also facing pollution because you drive right up to where they are when you go for a walk. To survive, the dark brown just before the tip turns into fluff to spread to make more cat tails in years to come.

To protect the cat tails we should give them more room to grow, move them away from the pollution and we will see many more. To protect where it lives there should be not any cars around so that it can live without pollution. No one should litter because it is hard for them to live with all the garbage so throw it in the garbage bins.

11 Math: Reaching All Learners in the Math Classroom

It Doesn't Have to Be a Four-Letter Word

This chapter has been contributed by Carole Saundry.

Ask anyone what their least favorite subject was in school and chances are they'll tell you it was math. The anxiety around finding the one right answer and doing it quickly disenfranchised so many learners that people simply believed themselves incapable of understanding mathematics. Rigid teaching methods—a quick demo of the procedure of the day, followed by pages of practice—made math incomprehensible to most children, or at best boring and irrelevant.

Filled with tricks and rules to remember, mathematics had evolved into a subject only few could understand, let alone master.

Notions of diversity traditionally have not extended into the math classroom; children who did not grasp the concepts were relegated to endless drill of the basic facts. In an effort to "simplify" content, students with learning difficulties were presented with "stripped down math," numbers on the page. Rarely did they engage in rich conceptual tasks.

We are learning to re-imagine math classrooms as places where students of all abilities work together on the same problem: a rich task focused on a concept worth revisiting over time. Real math is accessible to all members of the class community and different solution methods are honored and celebrated. The work of mathematician John Van De Walle has sculpted our thinking. His beliefs about mathematics learning parallel our view of literacy learning. To create the mathematics classes we want, Van de Walle states that we reconsider not just the tasks we present to students but the structure of the math lessons.

Reconsidering the Tasks

Tasks are focused on the math

Rather than practising more long division questions, intermediate students might consider these questions:

Tasks are about *concepts* (like "division as sharing") rather than procedures.

- When is it appropriate to divide a remainder into fractional pieces?
- When is a remainder negligible?
- In which contexts does having a remainder change the value of the quotient?
- Can you really rent 3.6 buses to go to the Aquarium?

These questions will help students understand that there are many different ways to divide and that each of the methods for division involves place value.

Tasks involve open-ended questions

If we ask "What is $380 \div 15$?" there is only one right answer—25 remainder 5 or 25.3333—and one assumed right method. Some students will find the answer effortlessly and be ready for another question quickly, while some will struggle with the algorithm, perhaps arriving at the right answer even without fully understanding the question or the processes involved.

If instead we ask, "How can you show 380 divided into 15 groups? How many different ways can you find? Show your thinking in numbers, pictures, and words," we invite students with different strengths to draw, build, or write about their ideas. Mathematical thinking is broadened and more accessible.

Tasks are contextualized

Rather than using traditional word problems, we have shifted to story problems. Here is an example:

> We'll be working with our little buddy class later this week to make craft stick rafts. The instructions we found show that each raft needs 15 sticks. We've gathered 380 sticks so far. Our little buddy class has 26 students. Will we have enough craft sticks to make rafts for everyone? How could you figure this out? Show your thinking in at least 2 different ways.

This context asks students to solve a division-by-grouping problem, to assess the meaning of the remainder, and to show more than one way to solve the problem. This is a rich task, one that all students in an intermediate classroom can access, even if it means counting out 380 craft sticks and making groups of 15. But consider how much you could learn about your students' conceptual understanding by asking this complex question instead of presenting them with $380 \div 15$.

Reconsidering the Lesson Structure

Like our literacy lessons, our math lessons are 60 to 90 minutes long. This allows time for the stages of the lesson. Like our literacy lessons, the stages are

- beginning (connecting)
- during (processing)
- after (personalizing/transforming)

A typical lesson structure might go this way:

BEFORE (CONNECTING) Stage-setting and connection-making A question, quick problem, or reminder of previous learning	5–10 minutes
DURING (PROCESSING) Presentation of the day's task Students explore and investigate a new, connected problem	20–30 minutes

AFTER (PERSONALIZING/TRANSFORMING)	
Strategy sharing and consolidation	10–20 minutes
Time to compare solutions and strategies, and to share thinking	
Reflection and practice	20–30 minutes
Writing or drawing to explain key learning; applying learning to new situations	

Introducing Division

Notice the power of the teacher's talk and the focus on student thinking and building understanding.

In this Grades 5/6 class, in just one lesson, a significant shift occurs in the students' use of precise math language and in their conceptual understanding of division. In co-planning for the lesson, the classroom teacher, Liz Nasu, has told me (her resource teacher) that the students' understanding of place value was not strong. Together we established the goals for the lesson:

- to introduce division in a visual, non-algorithmic way
- to address and build place-value concepts through problem-solving
- to develop mathematical language (specifically around division)
- to engage all learners

Before (Connecting)

We began the lesson by generating some vocabulary around division. We put an equation on the board and asked if students could guess what the lesson of the day was going to address. They quickly guessed division and pointed out that the clues were the division sign and the R3 for "Remainder 3." We labeled these items and prompted them for another name for remainder.

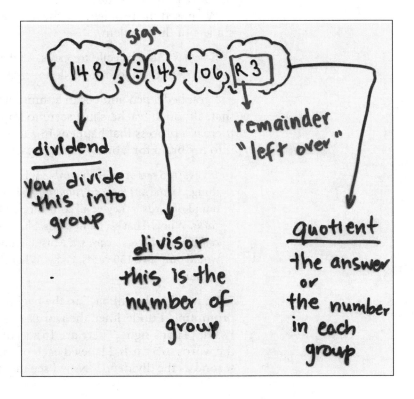

It is important for students to gain control over this specific language (dividend, divisor, quotient). New math textbooks and provincial assessments emphasize the power of math language in decoding problems and in communicating understanding.

After each child was finished, I took a digital photo of them and how the manipulatives had changed.

Since the specific vocabulary of division had not surfaced, we circled the other numbers in the equation. We asked the students to work in their groups to come up with the proper names for each of the terms—but that they should also think of a way to describe these terms to someone much younger. They worked in their groups. The mathematical language they shared and called up was rich—students made connections to prior grades, other lessons, and to places they might find this kind of language used.

During: Modeling

As it was just after Halloween, we used a related math problem. My son and I had been trick-or-treating and needed to share our 124 candies with 4 people. Some students used mental math and quickly shouted out that everyone should get 31 candies. We agreed, but reminded them that my son was only 8 and would not believe this unless we could show him how we arrived at 31 as a number.

I used base-ten blocks on the overhead and built 124 with one flat of 100, 2 rods of ten, and 4 singles. "Okay," I said, "I have the dividend 124. What should I do next?" Cara volunteered the next step, suggesting I break the 100 flat up into tens so I could share the pieces. I wrote her idea down in words on the overhead, then invited her to come to the overhead and show me how to do that. Cara traded the 100 for 10 tens and placed them on the overhead. The next student, Jordan, said that I should "Take the tens and make four groups." I wrote his directions on the overhead and had him come up and model his idea.

We continued, recording student language and movement of the manipulatives until the quotient was found. I confirmed for them that my son would believe this series of instructions, that it was clear and also showed how they had arrived at 31 as the answer.

We posed the problem for the day, selecting a student from the class as the subject of the problem.

Ji Ye has 15 sets of collector cards. All the sets have an equal number of cards. Ji Ye has 375 cards. How many collector cards are in each set?

I grabbed a pen and began a think-aloud for the problem. I told the students that, although teachers just seem to know how to solve problems, that actually there is a process that happens in a teacher's brain each time. "Let me let you into my brain for a bit..." I said. I started to doodle and draw on the overhead.

Ji Ye has 15 sets of collector cards. Hmm. Maybe they're like hockey cards or something. *All the sets have an equal number of cards.* Oh, okay. They must all be the same brand of cards—they've all come in packages like in tens or something. *Ji Ye has 375 cards.* Whoa. That's a lot of cards. She's been collecting for a while. *How many collector cards are in each set?* Must be more than ten in a set, because 15 sets of 10 would only give 150 cards. Okay. What should I do first? Let's see. What do I know for sure?

I paused and went back to the beginning of the problem. At the students' prompting, I underlined the words *15 sets* and wrote this below the problem. I said, "That's right. There are 15 sets of card all together." Next, I underlined the words *375 cards.* I labeled each of these terms, the first as the divisor and the second as the dividend. "Now I see that there's a question here that needs answering. It wants to know how many collector cards are in a set. I wonder how I could figure that out. I know that the dividend tells me how many cards there are all together—and the divisor tells me how many are in a group." I asked students to sort out which of the numbers in the problem was the dividend and which was the divisor. *What are we supposed to find?* I asked. "The answer," said one student. I prompted some more. "I mean the quotient," he corrected himself. "That means we'll have to divide."

During: Processing

I turned to the students and told them that I wanted them to solve this problem in their groups. They would have base-ten blocks to work with. They should record their process while they worked. They were to share the recording job so that everyone had a chance to record a stage of the de-constructing of the whole.

Each group was given a digital camera to photograph the stages of the process. This was a critical piece of the lesson's goals—to experience many different ways to divide and to highlight the notion that all division relies on place-value understanding. The cameras allowed students across the spectrum the chance to contribute to the final product, and to focus in on the manipulation of the base-ten materials. We were trying to appeal to the visual-spatial learners in the group and to provide for them a physical model for the mental process capable mathematicians use when doing mental division.

Student Work

Students fell to the task quickly. They established how many blocks they needed to start with, and who would be "on" with the camera first. As we wandered around the room, we prompted for mathematical language. "What is the dividend? How did you build it?" We encouraged students to use this specific language in their recordings.

Trading for tens was a fairly evident next step, but then when students were left with 75 blocks (7 tens and 5 singles) to share among the 15 groups, many stopped and had conversations with their peers to establish what to do next. "You can share out the tens evenly. You have to break them all up into singles first. Make an exchange. That'll be 75 singles." We teachers connected at the back of the room and celebrated the place-value language being used.

The Commercial Break: establishing criteria and problem solving

The classroom was noisy and busy—cameras flashed and materials were being assembled and disassembled. We stopped the students midway through the task for a "commercial break" and held up some student work. "I notice that this group is including key words in their work. Listen to this statement—it is clear what happened in this step."

We invited another group to share the problem they were having with their solution. There were 15 groups of 24 blocks and 9 leftover blocks to one side. "I think we lost some," Rachel mused. "There's not enough to go around." The other members of her group looked befuddled. They knew there had to be an equal number in each group because the question said so. We asked, "Is there a way you could figure out how many you have? Does anyone have a suggestion

Our thinking in having students use the digital camera was to force them to stop and record each stage as it was performed, and to be mindful of the process they were undertaking as they went.

Students with more verbal-linguistic capacity helped those who struggled to write and record the step when it was their turn.

Modeling students' use of language helps to spark other children's thinking and helps to clarify the expectation midway through the task.

for Rachel and her group?" Someone pulled out a calculator and wandered over to help. We ended the break and students began working again. Rachel and Sean sorted out how many cubes they had by multiplying 15 x 24 and adding the 9 leftover single blocks. "We only have 369 blocks," Rachel said, then counted on her fingers. "We need 1, 2, 3, 4, 5, 6 more." This kind of error analysis and self-correction told us a lot about Rachel and Sean's thinking about division and its relationship to multiplication.

Step 1: We made the dividend with 3 blocks of a hundred, 7 blocks of ten, and 5 singles.

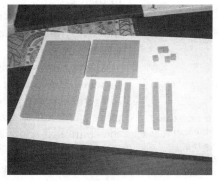

Step 2: We broke up the hundreds into tens. We had 30 tens, and 7 tens from before, plus 5 singles.

Step 3: We put the 30 tens into 15 sets.

Step 4: We turned the 7 tens that were left over into singles. We took the 75 singles and put them into 15 groups of 4.

Step 5: We realized that we could add one more to each group.

Step 6: We made 15 groups of 25, with 2 tens and 5 ones in each group.

After: Personalizing and Transforming

Strategy Sharing and Consolidation

As the class drew to a close, students had a chance to share their solutions, their strategies for solving the problem, and any difficulties that came up for them. Some made connections to Rachel's group's loss of pieces, and talked about how they figured out how many pieces there should be in the each set of collector cards. We talked about the method they had used to find the quotient, and how in each case it involved breaking up hundreds, tens, and singles. We took one group's collaborative work and read it, then modeled a way to record their thinking.

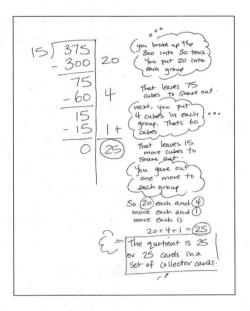

You started with a dividend of 375 and a divisor of 15. Let's write that down. We recorded in the way students normally structure a traditional long-division algorithm, but instead made connections to the actual movement of the materials and the place value work the students had done. Making the connection between how we solved it and how we might represent it is critical for students. To conclude the lesson, we summarized what we had learned and set the stage for using their new knowledge.

> "There are lots of ways to divide—using mental division, using base-ten materials to model the problem, using the repeated subtraction method for representing the process. All of these methods depend on place value—how we use ones, tens, and hundreds. Next week we'll have the chance to practise these and more strategies for division."

After: Reflecting and Practice

The next day, Liz asked her students to write about the task. One ESL student responded as follows:

> The troubles I had is that I could easily do the operation in my head, but it was hard for me to put into words and steps because I didn't remember doing math division that kind of way so it was neat to me. Another trouble I had was that I was confused

The method shown is one featured in many new math programs and is a far more sensible algorithm for representing and communicating the act of dividing. As a process, it relies on meaning and is whole-number based rather than a digit-based operation like traditional long division.

with the steps because for example 30 divided by 5. I builded the number and broke the 100 into tens, and 3 tens into 30 ones. Then it was confusing because I did not know if you put that 2 broke up tables into steps or ones. But the rest I thought was easily to understand:

As practice and consolidation, students were asked to use any method they wanted to in solving a range of division problems—some involving remainders, some without.

It is important to recognize that the volume of practice is not what we have been used to. Six questions were assigned to each grade level in this combined-grade classroom (Grade 6 students worked on the same concept but with thousands rather than hundreds).

- Only three questions were presented.
- Two additional problems were word problems requiring students to read and determine the dividend and divisor in each case before solving the problem.
- The final problem was more open ended and complex: students were given a quotient; for example "13 R 6." They were asked to explain what the dividend and divisor might be in each case, and then to explain their thinking. This "reverse procedure" question provided challenge for learners at the upper end of the spectrum, who were encouraged to explain how they had chosen their dividend and divisor, and what patterns they could see when comparing multiple solutions. Likewise, it was accessible to other students who could build and visualize a more simple solution—and still achieve the learning goals for the lesson.

The Big Ideas

Liz and I talked after the lesson. We commented on the time we took with our in-class math explorations, and our initial worry about assigning fewer practice problems. But then, we reflected on the students' increased understanding of the content and of their ability to communicate their thinking. This is the making of mathematicians.

Conclusion: Pulling It All Together

Our classrooms are richer, more vibrant learning spaces when all students are included. Although a diverse group of students may indeed pose more challenges to us as teachers, overcoming these challenges is not out of our reach. As teachers, we plan with the class in mind and make adaptations and modifications, as necessary, for individual students or small groups of students; we do not start with all our individual students and their special needs and attempt to make a class plan. We believe that our students have more in common rather than less in common. We believe that they want to be with us in the regular classroom and that they all want to belong. In order to belong, they must be involved in the academic curriculum as well as the social curriculum. We are challenged to know each of our students and our curriculum, and to use our skills to marry these as best we can. This requires knowing what our students can do, knowing what our students need to be able to do, choosing a focus for learning, designing a plan to achieve this focus, and being explicit with our learning goals.

Collaboration is key. Working alone, none of us is as fine an educator as we can be. Being a member of a learning team—with a resource person, a librarian, an administrator, another classroom teacher—is the first step in refining our professional skills. We have tried to model in our lessons the collaborative efforts of teams of teachers, of our best teaching when we are working with others. In our experience, having the opportunity to work side-by-side with another teacher in the classroom, for even a small amount of time, enriches our teaching and benefits all students. Students with special needs—identified or not—can receive support connected to their learning goals with the curriculum. We learn from having the opportunity to observe the interactions of another professional, even while teaching ourselves. When not working within the classroom, we prize co-planning lessons and units. The powerful conversations that occur in co-planning, reflecting, and analyzing student work energize us and propel us on to new learnings.

Assessment has taken on new meanings for us. We have shifted more and more from an emphasis on using data for reporting out progress, to using data to inform our instruction and our students' learning. This shift has helped us become more explicit in designing our teaching lessons, which has, in turn, caused a more profound growth in our students' achievement. We work to include our students in our assessment conversations, since they are the most in need of the information. They are learning to ask, "What do I need to be able to do? What can I do now? What support will I need to learn? How will I know when I have achieved this goal?" This is a critical stance for them to take throughout their lives, as these questions are those that fuel our learning.

To learn well, students need to feel emotionally safe and to be actively engaged. In planning our lesson sequences and our thematic units, we keep in mind the need to be constantly building strong classroom communities where all students do feel safe and can take risks in their learning. We "walk the talk," prizing differences and demonstrating how much more we learn through these differences. We are also keenly aware of the importance of engagement. To this end, we try to employ strategies that will address different styles and preferences for learning—working with words, with drawing, with models, inside and outside the classroom—prodding students into activity.

Over the years, we have witnessed the loss of voice and choice for students in school, especially as they move through the years. We believe that voice and choice are critical elements for inviting learners into learning. Voice and choice are the foundation of classroom structures like Writers Workshop and Literature Circles. They are celebrated in strategies such as Quadrants of a Thought and dialogue journals. They are possible in daily assignments where criteria have been established for the product or performance, and where a variety of ways are presented to display learning. Everybody can be collectively involved in learning without everybody doing exactly the same thing. It is this stance that ensures that everyone is learning to the best of his/her ability.

Deep learning, learning that stays with us and is mulled around in our minds, grows as a result of connections. Through all that we do—in planning for learning and in our interactions with our students—we thread the theme of connections. We use personal connections to introduce a new theme or unit, personal and text connections to make sense of and process new information, and personal, text, and world connections to transform and personalize new understandings. And we use the same thread of connections to help students build personal repertoires of learning strategies, ways of thinking and learning, that they can use independently of us.

All of this takes time. To profoundly affect student learning requires deep, thoughtful conversation and activity, involvement, and time. We are in a rush to be the best teachers we can be, but we are not in a rush to hurry students through a curriculum without their becoming lifelong, passionate, inquisitive learners.

Finally, we believe that there is no one right way. We have tried to present a sampling of exemplary classroom practices from very diverse classrooms where all students are learning. We present these to you as examples, as models, but not as one right answer. Your very best results will occur when you do as we have done: learn with each other, ask questions about one another's approaches, keep an active mental model of learning in your mind, and use your experiences, your professional learning community, your students, and your reflections to move you on to new possibilities.

Bibliography

Professional Literature

Allington, Richard (2004) LOMCIRA Fall Conference, Vancouver, BC.

Atwell, Nancie (1998) *In the Middle: New Understandings About Writing, Reading, and Learning, 2nd Ed.* Portsmouth, NH: Heinemann.

Atwell, Nancie (2002) *Lessons That Change Writers.* Portsmouth, NH: Heinemann.

Beers, K. (2002) *When Kids Can't Read—What Teachers Can Do.* Portsmouth, NH: Heinemann.

Biancarosa, G., & Catherine E. Snow (2004) *Reading Next: A Vision for Action and Research in Middle and High School Literacy: A report to Carnagie Corporation of New York.* Washington, DC: Alliance for Excellent Education.

British Columbia Ministry of Education, Skills and Training (1996) *English Language Arts K to 7. Integrated Resource Package.* Victoria, BC.

British Columbia Ministry of Education, Skills and Training (1996) *English Language Arts 8-10. Integrated Resource Package.* Victoria, BC.

British Columbia Ministry of Education and Ministry Responsible for Multiculturalism and Human Rights (1994) *Evaluating Reading Across Curriculum: Using the Reading Reference Set to Support Learning and Enhance Communication.* Victoria, BC.

British Columbia Ministry of Education and Ministry Responsible for Multiculturalism and Human Rights (2002) *B. C. Performance Standards for Reading and Writing, revised edition.* Victoria, BC: Student Assessment and Program Evaluation Branch. Retrieved November 1, 2005 from http://www.bced.gov.bc.ca/perf_stands/.

Brownlie, F. (2004) *Grand Conversations, Thoughtful Responses.* Winnipeg, MB: Portage & Main Press.

Brownlie, F., C. Feniak & V. McCarthy (2004) *Instruction and Assessment of ESL Learners: Promoting Success in Your Classroom.* Winnipeg, MB: Portage & Main Press.

Brownlie, F. & King, J. (2000) *Learning in Safe Schools.* Markham, ON: Pembroke.

Brownlie, F. (2004) *Literacy in the Middle Years: Part 1*, webcast. Retrieved December 5, 2005, from http://www.bced.gov.bc.ca/literacy/webcast.htm.

Brownlie, F. (2005) *Literacy in the Middle Years: Part 2*, webcast. Retrieved December 5, 2005, from http://www.bced.gov.bc.ca/literacy/webcast.htm.

Brownlie, F. & S. Close (1988) *Reaching for Higher Thought.* Scarborough, ON: Nelson Canada.

Butler, D. L., L. Schnellert, & S.C. Cartier (2005) "Adolescents' Engagement in 'Reading to Learn': Bridging from Assessment to Instruction" *BC Educational Leadership Research, 2.* Retrieved December 2, 2005, from http://slc.educ.ubc.ca/eJournal/index.htm>http://slc.educ.ubc.ca/eJournal/index.htm.

Davies, A., C. Cameron, C. Politano & K. Gregory (1992) *Together Is Better. Collaborative Assessment, Evaluation and Reporting.* Winnipeg, MB: Peguis.

Fielding, L. & D. Pearson. (1994) "Reading Comprehension: What Works." *Educational Leadership*, Vol. 51, #5.

Fogarty, R. (1997) *Problem-Based Learning and Other Curriculum Model for the Multiple Intelligences Classroom.* Arlington Heights, Illinois: Skylight Publishing.

Fogarty, R. (1990) "People Search" Workshop presentation. Richmond, BC: Thoughtful Cooperative Learning Workshop.

Gregory, K., C. Cameron & A. Davies (1997) *Setting and Using Criteria.* Merville, BC: Connections Publishing.

Jeroski, S. & F. Brownlie (2006) *Reading and Responding, Evaluation Resources for Teachers (grades 4, 5, and 6).* Scarborough, ON: Nelson Canada.

Morrow, Keyes, Johnson, et al. (2006) *Math Makes Sense - Grade 6 Western edition.* Toronto, ON: Pearson.

McGee, L. (1996) "Grand Conversations as Social Contexts for Literary Work." New York, NY: Paper presented at the American Education Research Association Conference.

Rose, David H. & Anne Meyer (2002) *Teaching Every Student in the Digital Age: Universal Design for Learning.* Alexandra, VA: ASCD.

Rothstein, Vicki & Rhoda Termansen (1999) *Language Learning Through Literature.* Austin, TX: PRO-ED.

Short, K. (1990) "Creating a Community of Learners" in *Talking About Books: Creating Literate Communities.* Portsmouth, NH: Heinemann.

Spandel, V. & R.J. Stiggens (1990) *Creating Writers.* New York, NY: Longman.

Tovani, Cris (2004) *Do I Really Have to Teach Reading?: Content, Comprehension, Grades 6-12.* Portland, ME: Stenhouse Publishers.

Van de Walle, John (2004) *Elementary and Middle School Mathematics: Teaching Developmentally.* Toronto, ON: Pearson.

Van de Walle, John & LouAnn Lovin (2006) *Teaching Student-Centered Mathematics: Grades 5–8.* Toronto, ON: Pearson.

Wells, G. (1986) *The Meaning Makers. Children Learning Language and Using Language to Learn.* Portsmouth, NH: Heinemann.

Wilhelm, Jeff (2001) *Improving Comprehension with Think Aloud Strategies: Modeling What Good Readers Do.* New York, NY: Scholastic.

Wilhelm, Jeff, Tanya Baker & Julie Dube (2001) *Strategic Reading: Guiding Students to Lifelong Literacy, 6–12.* Portsmouth, NH: Heinemann.

Children's Literature

Aiken, Joan. *Midnight Is a Place.* Boston, MA: Houghton Mifflin, 2002.

Aliki. *Painted Words, Spoken Memories.* New York, NY: Greenwillow, 1998.

Avi. *Crispin.* New York, NY: Hyperion, 2002.

Babbitt, Natalie. *Tuck Everlasting.* New York, NY: Farrar, Straus and Giroux, 1975.

Bradby, Marie. *More Than Anything Else.* New York, NY: Orchard, 1995.

Cherry, L. *The River Ran Wild.* New York, NY: Harcourt Brace Jovanovich, 1992.

Collier, J & C. *Jump Ship to Freedom.* New York, NY: Dell, 1987.

Cutler, Jane. *The Cello of Mr. O*. New York, NY: Dutton Children's Books, 1999.

D'Adamo, Francesco. *Iqbal*. New York, NY: Atheneum/Simon and Shuster, 2003.

Dickens, Charles. *Oliver Twist*. New York, NY: Tor Classics, 1994.

Doherty, Berlie. *Street Child*. London, UK: Collins, 1995.

Duncan Edwards, Pamela. *Barefoot*. New York, NY: Harper Collins, 1998.

Ellis, Deborah. *The Breadwinner*. Toronto, ON: Groundwood, 2001.

Ellis, Deborah. *The Heaven Shop*. Markham, ON: Fitzhenry and Whiteside, 2004.

Ellis, Deborah. *Mud City*. (sequel) Toronto, ON: Groundwood, 2004.

Ellis, Deborah. *Parvana's Journey*. (sequel) Toronto, ON: Groundwood, 2003.

Filipovic, Z. *Zlata's Diary*. New York, NY: Penguin, 1994.

Frank, A. *The Diary of Anne Frank*. New York, NY: Simon and Schuster, 1952.

Greenberg, Polly. *O Lord, I Wish I Was a Buzzard*. New York, NY: Seastar Books, 2002.

Haddix, Margaret Peterson. *Among the Hidden (Shadow Children #1)*. New York, NY: Aladdin, 2000.

Haskins, Jim. *Get On Board: The Story of the Underground Railroad*. New York, NY: Scholastic, 1997.

Heide, Florence Parry & Judith Heide Gilliland. *Sami and the Time of the Troubles*. New York, NY: Clarion, 1992.

Heneghan, James. *The Grave*. Toronto, ON: Groundwood Books/Douglas and McIntyre, 2000.

Ho, Minfong. *The Clay Marble*. New York, NY: Farrar, Straus and Giroux, 2003.

Kaplan, William. *One More Border*. Vancouver, BC: Douglas & McIntyre, 1998.

Kidd, Diana. *Onion Tears*. New York, NY: Harper Trophy, 1993.

Kogawa, Joy. "Hiroshima Exit" In *Themes on the Journey*, Barry James, ed. Scarborough, ON: Nelson, 1989.

Kositsky, Lynne. *A Mighty Big Imagining*. Toronto, ON: Penguin, 2001.

Kositsky, Lynne. *Rachael: The Maybe House*. Toronto, ON: Penguin, 2003.

Laird, E. *Kiss the Dust*. London, UK: Mammoth, 1991.

Laird, Elizabeth. *Secret Friends*. London, UK: Hodder Children's Books, 1996.

Laird, Elizabeth. *The Garbage King*. London, UK: Macmillan Children's Books, 2003.

LeBox, A. *Salmon Creek*. Toronto, ON: Groundwood, 2002.

Lowry, L. *Number the Stars*. New York, NY: Bantam, 1989.

Lyons, Mary E. *Letters from a Slave Girl*. New York, NY: Scribner, 1992.

Macken, Walter. *Flight of the Doves*. London, UK: Macmillan Children's Books, 2001.

Martin, Ann. *Belle Teal*. New York, NY: Scholastic, 2005.

Mikaelsen, Ben. *Petey*. New York, NY: Hyperion, 1998.

Mikaelsen, Ben. *Touching Spirit Bear*. New York, NY: Harper Collins, 2001.

Naidoo, Beverley. *Journey to Jo'burg*. New York, NY: Harper Trophy, 1988.

Naidoo, Beverley. *No Turning Back*. New York, NY: Harper Trophy, 1999.

Nye, Naomi Shihab. *Habibi*. New York, NY: Simon Pulse, 1999.

Palermo, Sharon. *The Lie That Had To Be*. Saskatoon, SK: Thistledown Press, 1995.

Park, Linda Sue. *A Single Shard*. New York, NY: Yearling, 2001.

Paterson, Katherine. *Jip: His Story*. New York, NY: Penguin, 1998.

Paulson, Gary. *Sarny: A Life Remembered*. New York, NY: Delacorte Press, 1997.

Pearson, Kit. *Awake and Dreaming*. Toronto, ON: Penguin, 1997.

Ringgold, Faith. *Aunt Harriet's Underground Railroad in the Sky*. New York, NY: Crown Publishers, 1992.

Sterling, D. *Freedom Train, The Story of Harriet Tubman*. Toronto, ON: Scholastic, 1954.

Sterling, S. *My Name Is Seepeetza*. Vancouver, BC: Douglas and McIntyre, 1992.

Watkins, Yoko Kawashima. *My Brother, My Sister and I.* (sequel) New York, NY: Simon Pulse, 1996.

Watkins, Y.K. *So Far from the Bamboo Grove*. New York, NY: Beach Tree, 1986.

Whelan, G. *Goodbye, Vietnam*. New York, NY: Randam House, 1992.

Whelan, Gloria. *Homeless Bird*. New York, NY: Harper Trophy, 2001.

Williams, Laura. *Behind the Bedroom Wall*. Minneapolis, MN: Milkweed, 1996.

Winters, Janette. *Follow the Drinking Gourd*. New York, NY: Knopf, 1992.

Wright, B.R. *The Ghost of Popcorn Hill*. New York, NY: Scholastic, 1994.

Yolen, J. *The Devil's Arithmetic*. New York, NY Puffin, 1988.

Zhang, Ange. *Red Land Yellow River*. Vancouver, BC: Douglas & McIntyre, 2004.

Index